UNION INTERNATIONALE DES SCIENCES PRÉHISTORIQUES ET PROTOHISTORIQUES
INTERNATIONAL UNION FOR PREHISTORIC AND PROTOHISTORIC SCIENCES

PROCEEDINGS OF THE XV WORLD CONGRESS (LISBON, 4-9 SEPTEMBER 2006)
ACTES DU XV CONGRÈS MONDIAL (LISBONNE, 4-9 SEPTEMBRE 2006)

Series Editor: Luiz Oosterbeek

VOL. 23

Session C52

Cognitive Archaeology as Symbolic Archaeology

Edited by

Fernando Coimbra
George Dimitriadis

BAR International Series 1737
2008

Published in 2016 by
BAR Publishing, Oxford

BAR International Series 1737

Proceedings of the XV World Congress of the International Union for Prehistoric and Protohistoric Sciences
Actes du XV Congrès Mondial de l'Union Internationale des Sciences Préhistoriques et Protohistoriques

Outgoing President: Vítor Oliveira Jorge
Outgoing Secretary General: Jean Bourgeois
Congress Secretary General: Luiz Oosterbeek (Series Editor)
Incoming President: Pedro Ignacio Shmitz
Incoming Secretary General: Luiz Oosterbeek

Cognitive Archaeology as Symbolic Archaeology

ISBN 978 1 4073 0179 2

© UISPP / IUPPS and the editors and contributors severally and the Publisher 2008

Signed papers are the responsibility of their authors alone.
Les texts signés sont de la seule responsabilité de ses auteurs.

Contacts: Secretary of U.I.S.P.P. – International Union for Prehistoric and Protohistoric Sciences
Instituto Politécnico de Tomar, Av. Dr. Cândido Madureira 13, 2300 TOMAR
Email: uispp@ipt.pt, www.uispp.ipt.pt

The authors' moral rights under the 1988 UK Copyright, Designs and Patents Act are hereby expressly asserted.

All rights reserved. No part of this work may be copied, reproduced, stored, sold, distributed, scanned, saved in any form of digital format or transmitted in any form digitally, without the written permission of the Publisher.

BAR Publishing is the trading name of British Archaeological Reports (Oxford) Ltd. British Archaeological Reports was first incorporated in 1974 to publish the BAR Series, International and British. In 1992 Hadrian Books Ltd became part of the BAR group. This volume was originally published by Archaeopress in conjunction with British Archaeological Reports (Oxford) Ltd / Hadrian Books Ltd, the Series principal publisher, in 2008. This present volume is published by BAR Publishing, 2016.

Printed in England

BAR titles are available from:

BAR Publishing
122 Banbury Rd, Oxford, OX2 7BP, UK
EMAIL   info@barpublishing.com
PHONE +44 (0)1865 310431
FAX   +44 (0)1865 316916
www.barpublishing.com

NOTE OF THE SERIES EDITOR

The present volume is part of a series of proceedings of the XV world congress of the International Union for Prehistoric and Protohistoric Sciences (UISPP / IUPPS), held in September 2006, in Lisbon.

The Union is the international organization that represents the prehistoric and protohistoric research, involving thousands of archaeologists from all over the world. It holds a major congress every five years, to present a "state of the art" in its various domains. It also includes a series of scientific commissions that pursue the Union's goals in the various specialities, in between congresses. Aiming at promoting a multidisciplinary approach to prehistory, it has several regional or thematic associations as affiliates, and on its turn it is a member of the International Council for Philosophy and Human Sciences (an organism supported by UNESCO).

Over 2500 authors have contributed to c. 1500 papers presented in 101 sessions during the XVth world Congress of UISPP, held under the organisation of the Polytechnic Institute of Tomar. 25% of these papers dealt with Palaeolithic societies, and an extra 5% were related to Human evolution and environmental adaptations. The sessions on the origins and spread of hominids, on the origins of modern humans in Europe and on the middle / upper Palaeolithic transition, attracted the largest number of contributions. The papers on Post-Palaeolithic contexts were 22% of the total, with those focusing in the early farmers and metallurgists corresponding to 12,5%. Among these, the largest session was focused on prehistoric mounds across the world. The remaining sessions crossed these chronological boundaries, and within them were most represented the regional studies (14%), the prehistoric art papers (12%) and the technological studies (mostly on lithics – 10%).

The Congress staged the participation of many other international organisations (such as IFRAO, INQUA, WAC, CAA or HERITY) stressing the value of IUPPS as the common ground representative of prehistoric and protohistoric research. It also served for a relevant renewal of the Union: the fact that more than 50% of the sessions were organised by younger scholars, and the support of 150 volunteers (with the support of the European Forum of Heritage Organisations) were in line with the renewal of the Permanent Council (40 new members) and of the Executive Committee (5 new members). Several Scientific Commissions were also established.

Finally, the Congress decided to hold its next world congress in Brazil, in 2011. It elected Pe. Ignácio Shmitz as new President, Luiz Oosterbeek as Secretary General and Rossano Lopes Bastos as Congress secretary.

L.O.

TABLE OF CONTENTS

Introduction 1
Fernando Coimbra and George Dimitriadis

'In the eye of the beholder': a re-evaluation of passage tombs in
  the Irish Neolithic landscape through the integration of spatial,
  visibility and archaeoastronomical data 3
Frank Prendergast

Celestial symbols on Bronze Age archaeological finds in the Carpathian Basin 13
Emilia Pasztor

The "domestication" of the world into a house and a home: Cosmographic
  symbolism as a basic expression of the human mind 21
Michael Rappenglück

The ship and its symbolism in the European Bronze Age 27
Andrea Vianello

Cognitive archaeology, rock art and archaeoastronomy: interrelated disciplines 35
Fernando Augusto Coimbra

Space Syntax Analysis as Cognitive Approach to Prehistoric Mentality 41
George Dimitriadis

Neolithic Codes - A Different Approach of Cucuteni Woman
  (para-archaeological and para-medical meditative essay) 47
Romeo Dumitrescu

Symbolism within technology 51
Dragos Gheorghiu

Organisation d'un sanctuaire rupestre: les rochers de Creysseilles (Ardèche, France) 55
Philippe Hameau

Simbologie du Métal: un proposition de reflexion sur les depots du B.F. IIIb
  de la region P.A.C.A. 63
Davide Delfino

LIST OF FIGURES

Fig. 1.1. Geographic distribution of 232 Irish passage tombs (a)
and 39 tombs with passages aligned on other tombs or cairns (b) 4

Fig. 1.2. Extent of passage tomb clustering, classification and condition 6

Fig. 1.3. Alignment distributions for 128 Irish passage tombs 7

Fig. 1.4. Astronomical declinations for tombs aligned on other tombs
and cairns (trendline: moving average period 2) 9

Fig. 1.5. Scale-free visual framework of linked passage tombs and cairns 9

Fig. 2.1. The orientation of the graves at Tápé – Széntéglaégető, Hungary 15

Fig. 2.2. The orientation of faces of skeleton at site Tápé- Széntéglaégető, Hungary 16

Fig. 2.3. The orientations of the graves at site Tiszafüred – Majoroshalom, Hungary 16

Fig. 2.4. The orientations of graves to the sunrise or sunset of the burial day 18

Fig. 2.5. The orientations of graves with goods showing local influence 18

Fig. 4.1. Gobustan, (a) self-igniting fire at Lokbatan mud volcano,
© Bundesanstalt für Geowissenschaften und Rohstoffe (BGR);
(b) carved ships, © Malahat Farajova; (c) stone tambourine 28

Fig. 4.2. pyramid of Unas, (a) antechamber, west (left) and north (right) wall and
ceiling decorated with stars; (b) boat pits; (c) relief in the causeway, after Verner 29

Fig. 4.3. Aegean depictions of boats, (a) 'frying pan' from tomb 174, Chalandriani;
(b) boat from Middle Helladic potsherds from Aegina, after Siedentopf;
(c) carved ship at Folia, © HERAC, photograph by G. Dimitriadis............................. 30

Fig. 4.4. Nebra disk, © Landesamt für Denkmalpflege und
Archäologie Sachsen-Anhalt, phtograph by Juraj Lipták.. 31

Fig. 4.5. Map showing the area of cultural exchange of the aquatic bird symbol,
Hungary is on the top, Transylvania (2) was a probable area of intercultural
exchanges, Orsoya (1) in Thrace, where the aquatic bird appear in Late Bronze
Age contexts, and northern Greece (2), where exchanges between Mycenaeans,
Thracians and Transylvanians took place. © Microsoft Corporation,
© NAVTEQ, © NASA (satellite photograph) 33

Fig. 5.1. Inscription with a swastika used as a letter... 36

Fig. 5.2. Fireball (on the top) in *San* ritual scene. (After Ouzman) 38

Fig. 5.3. Rock of Botelhinha. The sunbeams enter the hole and highlight the engravings .. 38

Fig. 5.4. "The Astronomical Observatory", Armenia (after Martirosian, 1975).................. 38

Fig. 7.1. The assemblie of statues from Isaiia - *Balta Popii* (county of Iassy) 48

Fig. 7.2. The assemblie of statues from Poduri - *Dealul Ghindaru* (county of Bacau)........ 49

Fig. 7.3. Comparative representation of 21 days period and the 21 statues
from the site of Isaiia - *Balta Popii* 50

Fig. 9.1. a. Vue générale du site à partir d'une photographie aérienne : division des différents espaces ; b. Organisation sémantique du sanctuaire 56

Fig. 9.2. a. le rocher H7.4 : zone occidentale ; b. le rocher OR.07 : zone orientale ; c. le rocher OR.01, dit des Pieds du Diable : zone orientale ; d. l'un des corniformes du rocher H7.4 ; e. un moellon de basalte avec gravures linéaires 58

Fig. 10.1. Distribution des depots etudiès en la region P.A.C.A. 64

Fig. 10.2. Les phalères de Moriez (par Barge H. 2004) 66

Fig. 10.3. La parure avec ceinture de La Loubière (par Courtois J.C. 1960) 67

Fig. 10.4. Les grandspenentifs de Les Trouquets (par Courtois J.C. 1960) 68

LIST OF TABLES

Tab. 1.1. Catalogue of passage tombs (43) aligned on other tombs and cairns 8

Tab. 2.1. Different types of vessels with solar or astral decorations from the Tumulus culture cemetery of Tápé- Széntéglaégető, Hungary 17

Tab. 2.2. Different types of vessels with solar or astral decorations from the Tumulus culture cemetery of Tiszafüred-Majoroshalom, Hungary 19

Tab. 10.1. Les objects communes aux depots 65

INTRODUCTION

Fernando COIMBRA

Institute Land and Memory – Center for Superior Studies (Mação, Portugal)

George DIMITRIADIS

Director of the Hellenic Rock Art Center (Philippi, Greece), International Summer School European Prehistory (Sardinia, Italy)

Session C 52 tryed to focus on the importance of theory in archaeological research. The coordinators consider that a cognitive-processual approach is an excellent help when it's necessary to deal with prehistoric iconography. As Colin Renfrew already mentioned, it's important "to examine the ways in which symbols were used" (*in Towards a cognitive archaeology*, 1994). This statement provides an extremely useful methodology to research prehistoric symbolism with a scientific approach.

To attend the session's purposes we called the interested researchers to submit both theoretical and applied papers, in order to collect manifestations of the past mentality hidden in different archaeological remains such as schematic rock art, pottery, the spatial distribution of tumuli and general iconography, among other examples. We had the participation of ten researchers that presented the following articles:

'In the eye of the beholder': a re-evaluation of passage tombs in the Irish Neolithic landscape through the integration of spatial, visibility and archaeoastronomical data, by Frank Prendergast (Ireland). The author analyses the spatial distribution of passage tombs in Ireland, focusing on their location on prominent hilltops and the intervisibility with neighbouring monuments, the integration of spatial distribution patterns, visual perceptions, orientation patterns, and astronomically significant alignments.

The significance of the sun, moon and celestial bodies to societies in the Carpathian Basin during the Bronze Age, presented by Emilia Pasztor (Hungary). This researcher studies the astral decorations on various objects from different social groups and the relation that they have with the other features of the artefacts such as material, colour, shape, purpose of use, role in the burial custom, position in grave.

The "domestication" of the world into a house and a home: Cosmographic symbolism as a basic expression of the human mind, by Michael Rappenglück (Germany). The author presents an interdisciplinary approach to the cosmographic symbolism found in archaeological remains across cultures and epochs, arguing that it can give important information about the structure and development of the human mind. He refers that his research is done by applying the results and methods of different sciences, such as biology, anthropology, archeoastronomy and philosophy.

The ship and its symbolism in European prehistory, presented by Andrea Vianello (Italy), who analyses some symbolisms attached to the image of the ship in rock art.

Cognitive archaeology, rock art and achaeoastronomy: interrelated disciplines, by Fernando Coimbra (Portugal), where the author presents some theoretical considerations, regarding the interrelationship of the three mentioned disciplines. He concludes that rock art is a privileged field for studying cognitive archaeology, because it has a kind of "directness", since the engravings allow the contact with "images from ancient worlds as ancient human minds envisioned them" (Taçon & Chippindale *in* The Archaeology of Rock Art, 1998).

Space Analysis as Cognitive Approach to Prehistoric Mentality, by George Dimitriadis (Greece). This researcher studies the anthropomorphic territory as an expression of the dispositional collocation of tribal dwellings and the figurative composition on megalithic slabs as two different scale examples how the prehistoric man tryed to re-organize the space according to his mentality. He argues that Space is more important as human existence parameter than Time.

Fertility kits. A possible approach of the female representations in Precucuteni - Cucuteni cultures, presented by Romeo Dumitrescu (Romania). The author examines two "boxes" with twenty one female statues discovered at Isaiia and Poduri (Romania). After an analysis with a doctor's eye, he arrives to the conclusion that this group of artefacts could represent a schema of the fertile female period.

Symbolic technologies in Chalcolithic Clay Cultures, by Dragos Gheorghiu (Romania), who focuses on the symbolism of cyclical processes of construction of objects in the East European Chalcolithic clay cultures, arguing that those technologies could be activities with a high symbolic content besides their functional character.

Organisation d'un sanctuaire rupestre: les rochers de Creysseilles (Ardèche), by Philippe Hameau (France), who studies two groups of carved rocks with a different iconography and analyses those differences.

Simbologie du Métal: le cas des dépôts dans les Alpes de l'Ouest au Bronze Final, by Davide Delfino (Italy). This researcher studies the composition, geographic location and synchronic archaeological contexts of the deposits of metal artefacts in the mentioned area, in order to start a cognitive study to understand a possible symbology of power, of the sacred or other.

After the presentation of all of the papers there was a very productive discussion about the following subjects: Cognitive Processual Archaeology as a methodology for analysing symbolic representations in archaeology; primitive mentality; interdisciplinarity between Rock Art, Anthropology, Archaeoastronomy and Geology.

This discussion led to some conclusions: it's still necessary a research of contextual character to understand the impact of the sun in the ritual life during European Bronze Age; some presupposed "solar symbols" are not necessarily related with solar cults; it's important to study the day and night astronomical environment to understand some engraved rocks and megalithic monuments.

The Coordinators

'IN THE EYE OF THE BEHOLDER': SYMBOLISM AND MEANING IN IRISH PASSAGE TOMB ALIGNMENT AND HEIGHT

Frank PRENDERGAST

School of Archaeology, University College Dublin &
Department of Spatial Information Sciences, Dublin Institute of Technology

Abstract: This paper presents and documents the preliminary findings of an analysis of Irish passage tomb alignments at regional and national level. Field measurements of location, passage alignment, horizon characteristics, and visibility have revealed new and potentially significant distribution patterns in tomb alignment, their intervisibility and links. Many of the tombs are directed towards other tombs or cairns, and this phenomenon occurs across the whole geographic distribution range. Furthermore, evidence is presented that is indicative of an apparent and overwhelming trend of such tombs being directed at altitudinally higher monuments or locations. The cultural, phenomenological and ontological aspects of height are examined in the context of these findings.
Keywords: Archaeology, Neolithic, Irish passage tombs, Alignment, Height, Linked, Astronomy.

Résumé: Cet article présente et documente les résultats préliminaires d'une étude régionale et nationale d'alignement de tombeaux de passage. Des mesures de terrains portant sur l'emplacement des passages, leur orientation, leurs charactéristiques, et leurs connections ont révélé de nouveaux modèles potentiellement importants de distribution d'alignement de tombes, d'intervisibilité et de relations mutuelles. De nombreux alignements de tombeaux sont orientés directement vers d'autres tombes ou cairns, et ce phénomène se répète sur toute la répartition géographique. De plus, cette étude indique une tendance apparente de ces tombes à être majoritairement orientées en direction de monuments topographiquement plus élevés. Les aspects culturels, phénomenologiques et ontologiques associés aux relations topographiques sont examinés dans le contexte de ces résultats.
Mots Clés : Archéologie, Néolithique, Tombeaux de passage irlandais, Alignement, Altitude, Connections, Topographie, Astronomie

[If therefore, anyone genuinely desires to investigate the truth of things, he should not select one particular science: all of them stand together and are interdependent.]

René Descartes, 1628

INTRODUCTION

In any analysis of society, monumentality and landscape, the modern scholar might usefully refer to the urban and landscape planning requirements of developed societies that *inter alia* assess the visual impact of structures on the built or natural environment. Such requirements invariably require that proposed design schemes will incorporate aesthetic values, and reflect and respect the traditions of the society or community in which they are situated. It might reasonably be argued that the motivation for such ideals has a shared temporality and relevance for as long as man has lived in organised social groups.

The development of methodologies for the assessment of visual impact on landscape by new buildings in Smardon *et al* (1986: 38) for example, provide relevant commentary on the (arguably) immutable link between the human psyche and action *viz*.

[Throughout human history, people have struggled to understand their environment. The problem is not straightforward because our only direct means of experiencing contextual phenomena is through our senses… …The underlying assumption of all scenery analysis is that populations share common bases in how they 'see' and subsequently respond to various landscapes.]

Zube (1986: 17) offers three paradigms for landscape assessment - professional, behavioural and humanistic. His behavioural model draws on psychology to assess the responses of a participant positioned in a landscape. In the humanistic model, he draws on the traditions and methods of anthropology, cultural geography, history and phenomenology, in his attempts to understand the transactions between humans and landscape. In recent studies on the ancient Maya and other Mesoamerican peoples, Houston and Taube (2000) present evidence that could allow for the possibility of reconstructing the phenomenology of those societies. The intense interest in the senses by the Maya, especially sight and sightlines (as the consequence of seeing), meant that spaces and places could have been given "moral and hierarchical valuation" through visual fields. That argument is in part supported by the following verse from the 16th century Mayan *Popul Vuh* (or Book of the Community):

[And as they looked, their knowledge became intense. Their sight passed through trees, through rocks, through lakes, through seas, through mountains, through plains.]

Tedlock (1996: 147; Cit. par Houston and Taube, *ibid*.)

Aesthetics are in the eye of the beholder. The eye is a lens for the mind. The monuments that people build are and were preconceived within the conceptual schemes of the mind, and perhaps additionally influenced by the surrounding landscape, culture, cyclical astronomical events, prevailing social climate, and how groups self organised. In the following consideration of Irish passage tombs therefore, the height and alignment aspects of their

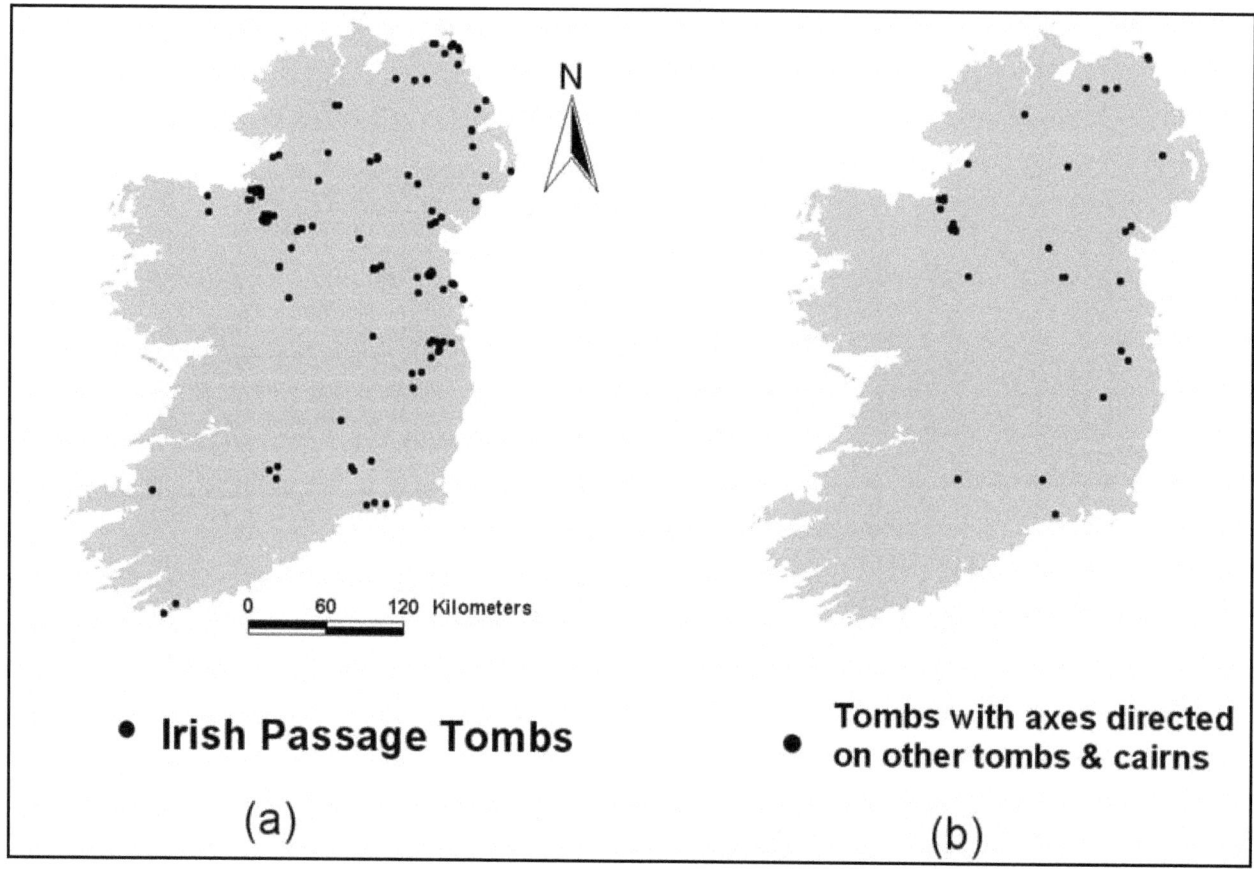

Fig. 1.1. Geographic distribution of 232 Irish passage tombs (a) and 39 tombs with passages aligned on other tombs or cairns (b).

design are positioned and considered within this psychological and cosmological framework in order to examine the possible significances of this culturally homogenous monument class in a symbolic, phenomenological and ontological context.

IRISH MEGALITHIC TOMBS AND THE PASSAGE TOMB TRADITION

Typological studies on Irish megalithic tombs have identified four distinctive classes - court, portal and passage tombs constructed during the Neolithic, and wedge tombs that belong mainly to the Bronze Age. Shee Twohig (2004: 9) has additionally identified a simple polygonal passage tomb type also belonging to the Neolithic. Each monument class has locational, morphological and depositional characteristics that allow such differentiation into these distinct and homogenous groups. The surveys and inventories of De Valera (1960), Herity (1974) and Ó Nualláin (1983: 113; 1989) indicate a total of *circa* 1,448 tombs on the island of Ireland, of which 391 are listed as court tombs, 174 as portal tombs, 229 as passage tombs and 465 as wedge tombs. A further 189 are listed as unclassifiable due to their poor condition. More recent published reports indicate an upward revision of the court tomb total to over 400 (Cody, 2002), and a smaller increase in the passage tomb total (*e.g.* Berg 1995: 225). Any future reconsideration and excavation of the numerous extant hilltop cairns could increase the passage tomb total further still (*e.g.* McGuinness, 1995). The currently known distribution of Irish passage tombs (232) is illustrated (based on GPS positioning by the author) in Figure 1.1a.

The varied morphology found in passage and other tomb types has led to the preferred use of the term 'tradition' within each class (*e.g.* Berg, *ibid*; Shee Twohig, 2004). Tombs of the court and passage tradition can be classified as long barrow-type monuments and are the subject of continued debate regarding their external and internal cultural influence and development, spatial relationships, cultural overlaps and chronologies. Herity (1974: 72) suggests an affinity for some of the Irish tombs on the east coast with the earlier tombs of southern Brittany. Corlett (1994: 12) argues "a combination of conflicting approaches is necessary to explain the origins of a variety of similar megalithic types that occur over a wide geographical area". His consideration of the anti-diffusionist *versus* the neo-diffusionist debate in an Irish context concludes that the anti-diffusionist approach regarded the motivation for tomb building as being inspired by "a radical reorganisation by local communities of their societies and economies due to the arrival of Neolithic economies and social organisation, and based very much on the spatial and chronological context of megaliths." In contrast, the neo-diffusionist approach was "essentially based on the morphological and conceptual aspects" of tomb building, and failed to accommodate "certain chronological issues" relating to the primacy of the passage tombs of Brittany and Iberia, for example. Thus both approaches failed to address the many issues raised by the spatial, conceptual, morphological and chronological contexts of the tombs.

The different tomb types clearly overlapped – chronologically, culturally and spatially (see De Valera 1960: 71; Cooney and Grogan 1999: 54). In addition, and when a tomb ceased to function as a burial site, its continued existence in the landscape may have held new meanings and imperatives for later generations of users and communities. New interpretations and cultural meaning could therefore be justifiably proposed and attributed, in addition to the ascribed primary use of the site and monument as a place for burial and ritual (Cooney and Grogan *ibid*; Ruggles 1999: 158; Shee Twohig 2004: 47).

Chronology

Notwithstanding the (controversial) outlying early dates obtained by Burenhult (1984) for certain tombs in the Carrowmore group in northwest Ireland, the majority of Irish passage tombs broadly date from *c*. 3400 BC to *c*. 2700 BC. Twelve dates were obtained from radiocarbon samples obtained in Tomb 51 at Carrowmore, of which eight indicate a limited time span for the construction and use of the central chamber. All fall within the period 3650 – 3450 BC (Burenhult, 1998). Radiocarbon (C^{14}) dates and their contexts have also been published for several of the tombs in the Boyne valley, and these similarly indicate a compressed chronology for tomb building activity in that region. Several phases of settlement and construction have been identified at Knowth for example, all occurring between *c*. 3500 BC and *c*. 3000 BC (Eogan & Roche, 1997). More recent excavation of the passage tomb at Tara, Co. Meath has yielded evidence of pre-cairn activity dating to 3707 cal. BC – 3521 cal. BC (1σ) based on C^{14} analysis of charcoal. Cremated bone found within the megalithic tomb yielded a radiocarbon determination of 3357 cal. BC – 3101 cal. BC (O'Sullivan, 2005). These data could offer support to the generally held thesis that passage tomb building began in the northwest of the island during the Early Neolithic and then spread south eastwards and to the Boyne valley, mostly during the Middle Neolithic. The increasing tomb complexity and sophistication over time, together with other evidence emanating from the material culture of the passage tomb tradition suggest that new imperatives were driving social and cultural change. Whether such a "transformation" (Eogan *c*. 1986: 213) evolved spontaneously from within the court tomb culture, or was the result of diffusion by new ideologies from the outside, remains a key question.

Monumentality, meaning and context

When considering the scale of monumentality to be found at some passage tomb sites, Cooney (*ibid*.) identifies 'focal tombs' that dominate the surrounding landscape because of their large size, and which have high visibility as a result of their deliberate siting on hilltops. The phenomenon does not appear to occur within the other classes of tomb. This focal characteristic suggests that specific tombs and places may have been imbued with special meaning and importance. Fraser (1998) additionally draws attention to the landscape resulting from the construction of such dominant tombs "as being gradually transformed from a meaningful locus which conceals within it the human efforts of monumental construction, to a landscape that derives its significance from massive summit cairns visible from considerable distances." Such concepts of materiality coexisting alongside new and different tomb building strategies could be the conesquence of people and communities being embedded in their own local landscapes and *vice versa*. Being situated in any one landscape, it is probable that the occupants would have been acutely conscious of distant but visible 'other sacred places' that were visually and symbolically linked, creating a nexus with possible ideological significances and meaning. It is also probable that such sights and sightlines could have held "the moral and hierarchical valuation through these visual fields", as previously stated.

Megalithic Art

The characteristic art inscribed on many of the structural stones of Irish passage tombs is the most concentrated, developed and significant of the Western European megalithic art tradition. With very few exceptions, such as the megalithic art on the roof-slab of the central tomb P51 of the Carrowmore group (probably a portal tomb but later modified into a passage tomb), all Irish megalithic art is confined to monuments of the passage tomb tradition. It is thus frequently argued that the passage tombs are the legacy of a hierarchical society, in contrast to the simpler social groups represented by the other tomb types. In an attempt to both widen and re-invigorate the debate on the meaning, symbolism and iconography of megalithic art, O'Sullivan (1997) argues for the introduction of the neuropsychological model of explanation to avoid possible distortions inherent in arguing from a single perspective.

Defining Criteria

Although the court and passage tombs share similar landscapes, chronologies and contexts to varying extents (Cooney, 2000: 112-119; Cody, 2002: 288) the latter class of monument differs distinctly from the other classes of tomb. Using interrelated and well defined criteria identified in discussions on Irish passage tomb cemeteries (Cooney, 1990: 742), it is evident that passage tombs and their covering cairns (though not all tombs are or were

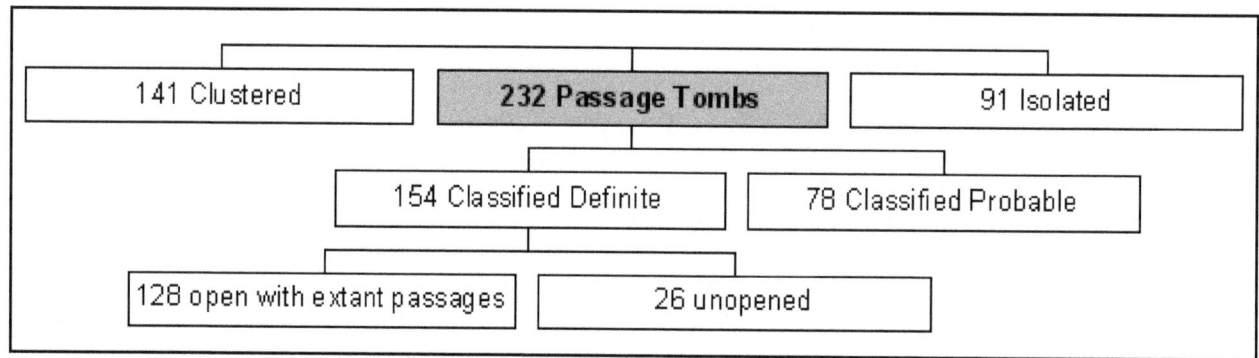

Fig. 1.2 Extent of passage tomb clustering, classification and condition.

covered) have attained large basal diameters and height in some instances, are mostly kerbed, are typically located in altitudinally high and intervisible locations, are often clustered in well defined areas termed 'cemetery' complexes with focal tombs, and have their passages aligned either towards other tombs or cairns, or astronomical markers on the horizon at culturally significant periods of the year.

Altitude, size and visibility

Altitude and visibility have been recognised by other researchers as possible factors behind the motivation to place passage tombs in landscapes that lie above the realm of normal settlement (*e.g.* McMann, 1994: 535). The "classic contrast" between the relatively low-lying and inconspicuously located court tombs in agriculturally more favourable soils, and the passage tombs that are prominently located on hilltops, is evident in Counties Donegal, Sligo and Wicklow for example (Cody, 2002: 287-289; Berg, 1995:130-135; Stout, 1994: 5). By placing a tomb in an upland area (with its probable lower density of tree cover), and by increasing the volume of material in the cairn covering the tomb, a dramatic 'visual signature' would have been created for those living in the local landscape below or beyond the area. This suggests a more complex symbolism and meaning than is encountered in the other types of tomb. Kilfeather (1997: 93) refers to the separation of the environment of the living from places that held the dead, and importantly points to the "defined links" that might have been achieved through the use of intervisible places at high altitude (see also Tilley, 1994: 156). Prendergast (forthcoming) indicates both long-range visibility and a high degree of intervisibility to be a recurring theme throughout the entire distribution range of the Irish tombs.

SURVEY METHOD AND ANALYSIS

In order to investigate alignment and other phenomena potentially inherent in the Irish passage tombs, the research began in 2004 as a doctoral thesis. The aim was to first embark on a primary data gathering campaign that would encompass the geographically broadest distribution area of the Irish passage tomb tradition. Thus field visits to all 232 known passage tombs have been undertaken (Figure 1.1). An additional 32 (possibly related) hilltop cairns, and 11 (possibly related) tombs on the island of Anglesey, Wales, have been additionally included but these are excluded from this analysis and discussion, and Figure 1.1. This is now facilitating and enabling many strands and themes of meaningful enquiry, underpinned by the primacy of the very large data set that has been collected.

The extent of clustered *versus* isolated tombs, the number of tombs classified as definite or probable, and the number of tombs with accessible passages are illustrated in Figure 1.2. Tombs that are classified 'probable' are either badly damaged but exhibit sufficient of the classic features to permit inclusion in the passage tomb inventory, or are unopened cairns lying within the precinct of clustered tombs that are classified as 'definite' passage tombs.

Surveys were conducted at each monument to record current condition, location in 3D on the Irish Grid reference system, proximity of the horizon (360°) using three distance categories, indications of alignment on significant archaeology or topography on the horizon, tombs or cairns generally intervisible with the site, alignment (azimuth) of the passage axis, angular altitude of the horizon sector indicated or framed by the alignment of the passage, and a photographic record for inventory purposes.

A preliminary consideration of the alignment of 128 tombs with extant and thus accessible passages yields five apparent distributions in the alignments (Figure 1.3).

Category 1 alignments (39) indicate the recorded extent of tomb alignment, either on other prominent passage tombs or hilltop cairns. These phenomena form the principal focus of this paper, and are examined at the discussion stage. Category 2 alignments (21) indicate that a proportion of the tombs are aligned on potentially significant astronomical solar events on the horizon *i.e.* sunrise or sunset. These occur with varying precision and goodness of fit, as dictated by the physical condition of the tomb,

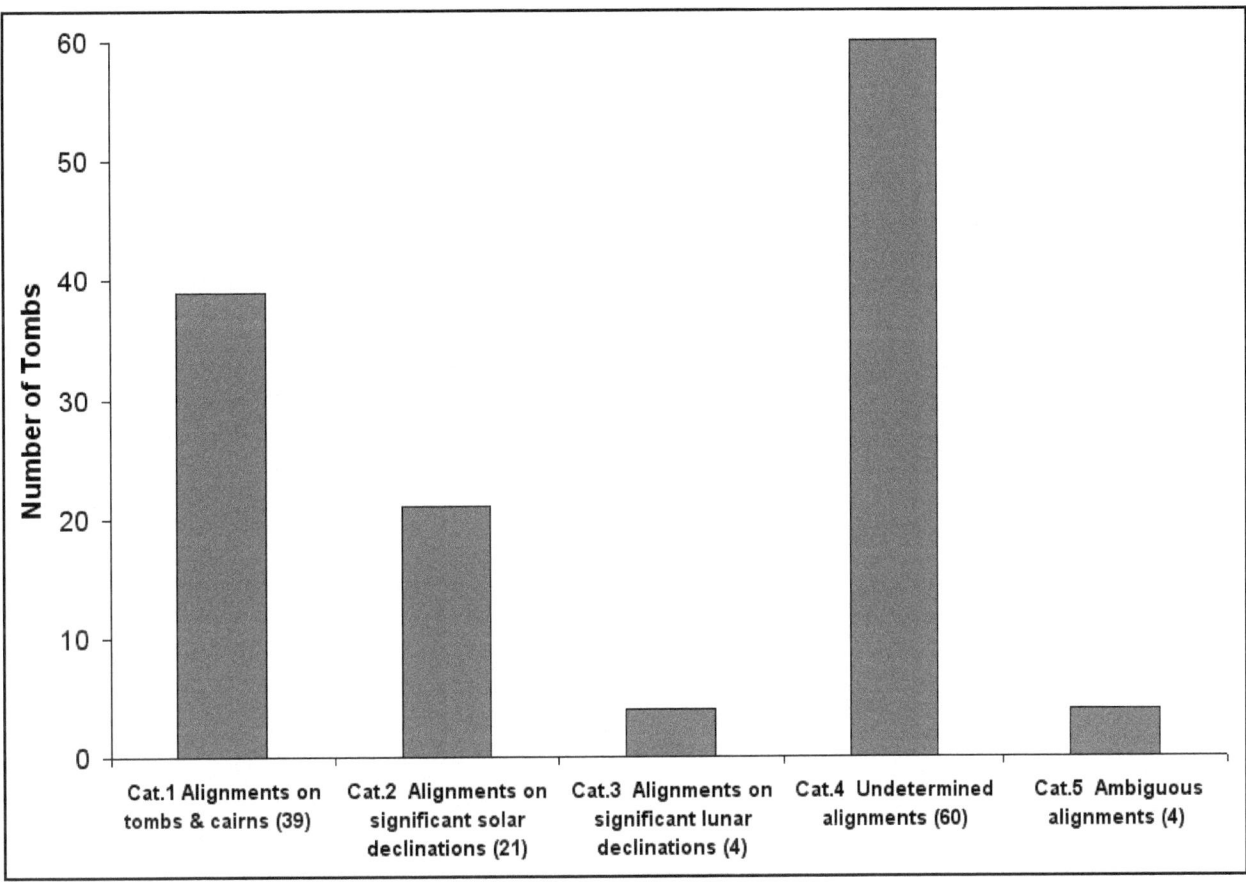

Fig. 1.3. Alignment distributions for 128 Irish passage tombs.

and the ability to discern the centreline axis of the passage based on the ratio of the passage width to its length. Category 3 alignments (4) have astronomical declinations that indicate possible alignment on significant lunar events on the horizon. The astronomical declinations were derived from the field survey data using algorithms developed by the author. Category 4 alignments (60) are as yet undetermined and represent the highest proportion of the sample and require further research into their potential significance, interpretation and any possible cultural meaning. Category 5 alignments (4) are those passage tombs that can be interpreted as orientated to both astronomically interesting declinations and a tomb or cairn. It is thus not possible to discern which phenomenon may be relevant, if any.

Examination of the spatial data for Category 1 alignments given in Table 1.1 and illustrated in Figure 1.1b, indicates that this phenomenon *i.e.* the alignment of tombs in column 1 (i denotes 'from') to tombs/cairns in column 2 (j denotes 'to'), is not restricted to any one region and extends over the whole geographical area of the passage tomb tradition (Figure 1.1b). The variation in range (distance) is from *c*. 250 metres to a maximum of *c*. 35 km and shows no clear preference for any particular range (indicated in a separate statistical analysis of the data being undertaken for the PhD thesis). In addition, and where such alignments do occur, the vertical spatial relationship is predominantly positive *i.e.* the tomb that is orientated towards another tomb or cairn is altitudinally below the tomb or cairn that is the apparent target of such an alignment *i.e.* they 'look upwards'. The catalogue in Table 1.1 includes the four tombs from Category 5 because three of these exhibit the same positive height difference in their vertical alignment relationship with the target tomb or cairn. Of the 43 alignments therefore, 38 (83%) are directed at tombs or cairns that are altitudinally higher.

The computed astronomical declinations for the Category 1 alignments indicate little evidence of an interest in solar astronomical alignments as indicated in the histogram and trend line (Figure 1.4). This could lend support to the hypothesis that site selection and the alignment of at least some of these tombs were motivated by the desire to face either higher places or spaces already regarded as sacred, or dominant 'focal' tombs or cairns already *in situ* at such locations. A more detailed consideration of these phenomena will follow in the thesis.

The data in Table 1.1 indicate that instances of multiple alignments (*i.e.* >1, ≤7) towards specific tombs or cairns occur at six locations in counties Antrim (An), Louth (Lh), Meath (Me), Longford (Lf) and Sligo (Sl). The gigantic cairn on Knocknarea mountain (Sl5) receives the highest number of hits (7) from tombs situated in the

Tab. 1.1. Catalogue of passage tombs (43) aligned on other tombs and cairns.

(i) Passage Tombs aligned on other tombs / cairns							(j) Passage Tombs & unclassified cairns linked to (i)								
1	2	3	Axis	4	5	6	7	8	9	Axis	10	11	12	13	14
Craigs	A	An 11	1	297401	417284	163	Drumsurn Upper	B	De 1	1	274325	417282	403	+	2.6
West Torr	A	An 8	1	321277	440640	298	Knocklayd	A	An 7	0	311521	436393	512	+	-11.0
Caranmore	A	An 9	1	321785	438779	379	Knocklayd	A	An 7	0	311521	436393	512	+	-5.8
Banagher	A	Cv 1	1	246680	299729	235	Corrstown (T)	A	Me 24	1	258617	277573	274	+	-31.5
Drumsurn Upper	B	De 1	1	274325	417282	403	Sl. Gallion	C	De 4	0	281300	389600	496	+	-33.9
Moneydig	A	De 2	1	288943	416550	49	Knocklayd	A	An 7	0	311521	436393	512	+	22.9
Kilmonaster (A)	A	Dg 1	1	227338	397621	77	Cloghroe	P	Dg 20	0	213400	400660	180	+	13.0
Kilmonaster (J)	A	Dg 10	1	227922	397399	89	Kilmonaster (L)	A	Dg 12	0	229938	397466	223	+	3.9
Finner (1)	A	Dg 16	1	183798	360423	36	Scrabbagh	B	Le 7	0	183350	352100	523	+	-31.9
Ballynahatty	A	Dw 1	1	332739	367700	46	Ballycollin	C	An 21	0	326113	370571	328	+	17.1
Crockaundreenagh	A	Du 9	1	301943	223721	346	Slievethoul 1	A	Du 7	0	301678	222879	397	+	-31.5
Baunfree	B	Kk 2	1	243023	128322	261	Temple Etney	C	Ti 2	0	229860	130732	721	+	-26.8
Deerpark	A	Li 1	1	177930	128391	270	Bolanlisheen/Templehill	B	Li 3	0	183310	121810	786	+	32.5
Ravensdale Park	A	Lh 1	1	309908	315755	508	Moyer	C	Cv 2	0	272190	295987	337	-	-15.4
Faughart Lw.	B	Lh 2	1	305302	312001	51	Ravensdale Park	A	Lh 1	1	309908	315755	508	+	24.2
Corstown (V)	A	Me 26	1	258671	277557	260	Corrstown (T)	A	Me 24	1	258617	277573	274	+	0.2
Monknewtown	B	Me 40	1	300905	275422	40	Dowth (A)	A	Me 41	1	302382	273767	73	+	5.9
Newtown (I)	A	Me 10	1	257190	277331	240	Corrstown (T)	A	Me 24	1	258617	277573	274	+	-6.3
Newtown (J)	A	Me 12	1	257166	277418	240	Newtown (L)	A	Me 14	1	257201	277408	240	+	-9.8
Newtown (K)	A	Me 13	1	257221	277431	240	Kingstown & Carnuff Gr.	C	Me 75	0	292575	269018	136	-	-8.6
Newtown (L)	A	Me 14	1	257201	277408	240	Kingstown & Carnuff Gr.	C	Me 75	0	292575	269018	136	-	21.9
Newtown (D)	B	Me 6	1	257044	277306	254	Kingstown & Carnuff Gr.	C	Me 75	0	292575	269018	136	-	-26.2
Sheegeragh (A)	B	Ro 4	1	184729	277979	73	Cornhill	C	Lf 1	0	218765	284220	278	+	6.0
Sheegeragh (B)	B	Ro 5	1	184734	278063	73	Cornhill	C	Lf 1	0	218765	284220	278	+	6.6
Ardloy	A	Sl 99	1	173737	316599	92	Knocknarea South	B	Sl 5	0	162604	334586	323	+	30.3
Barnashrahy	A	Sl 87	1	165974	335300	30	Carrownamadoo	A	Sl 95	1	170421	329574	217	+	-25.0
Carnaweeleen	B	Sl 97	1	171688	313222	242	Knocknarea South	B	Sl 5	0	162604	334586	323	+	-29.6
Carrowkeel (C)	A	Sl 104	1	174820	312094	270	Keshcorran/Murhy	B	Sl 96	0	171281	312629	361	+	5.4
Carrowkeel (D)	A	Sl 105	1	174829	312063	270	Carrowkeel (G)	A	Sl 108	1	175311	311940	300	+	-5.5
Carrowkeel (E)	A	Sl 106	1	174922	311616	320	Knocknarea South	B	Sl 5	0	162604	334586	323	+	31.1
Carrowkeel (F)	A	Sl 107	1	174939	311386	310	Carrowkeel (E)	A	Sl 106	1	174922	311616	320	+	36.2
Carrowkeel (G)	A	Sl 108	1	175311	311940	300	Knocknarea South	B	Sl 5	0	162604	334586	323	+	27.4
Carrowkeel (H)	A	Sl 109	1	175302	311869	305	Knocknarea South	B	Sl 5	0	162604	334586	323	+	20.7
Carrowkeel (K)	A	Sl 110	1	175335	311732	320	Knocknarea South	B	Sl 5	0	162604	334586	323	+	31.8
Carrowmore (P4)	A	SL 13	1	166241	333781	49	Carrowmore (P3)	A	Sl 11	1	166207	333740	52	+	-26.5
Geln / Croaghaun	A	Sl 93	1	163487	327512	176	Barroe North	B	Sl 103	0	180290	315494	228	+	-18.6
Knocknarea South	A	SL 7a	1	162781	334262	270	Mullanashee / Doonmor	A	Sl 116	0	160936	327412	270	+	-34.0
Treanmacmurtagh	B	Sl 100	1	173095	312183	247	Knocknarea South	B	Sl 5	0	162604	334586	323	+	32.3
Treanmore	B	SL 98	1	172503	312125	219	Keshcorran / Murhy	B	Sl 96	0	171281	312629	361	+	19.1
Sess Kilgreen	A	Ty 3	1	260407	358435	117	Shantavny Irish	A	Ty 6	1	260186	359691	171	+	38.6
Matthewstown	A	Wa 3	1	252916	102902	78	Seefin Mtn	C	Wa 4	0	227400	106800	725	+	6.8
Baltinglass (A)	A	Wi 14A	1	288551	189253	370	Tornant Upper	B	Wi 13	0	287462	199920	245	-	35.1
Seefin	A	Wi 6	1	307354	216263	621	Ballinascorney Upper (B)	A	Du 11	1	308146	219712	648	+	34.0

Columns 1, 7: Townland Name
Columns 2, 8: Tomb Classification (A=Definite Passage Tomb, B= Probable, C= Cairn or Possible Tomb, P=Portal Tomb)
Columns 3, 9: County / Project Code (after Herity 1974)
Columns 4, 10: Irish Grid Eastings (metres)
Columns 5, 11: Irish Grid Northings (metres)
Columns 6, 12: Height above Mean Sea Level (metres)
Column 13: Height Diff. (+) or (-)
Column 14: Astronomical Declination° ± 0°.5

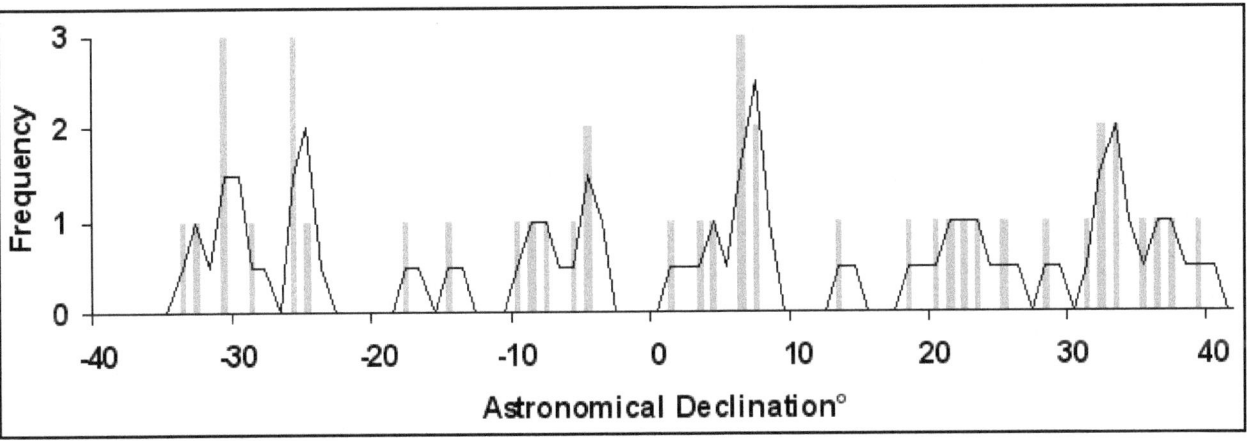

Fig. 1.4. Astronomical declinations for tombs aligned on other tombs and cairns (trendline: moving average period 2).

Carrowmore complex and surrounding landscape. The extent of this recurring phenomenon is graphically represented in Figure 1.5. In this scale free diagram, a framework has been constructed so as to clearly visualise the (apparent) links between the tombs. To overcome the difficulties imposed by using a true scale plot to represent the tombs that are linked but which have a large variation in range (*c.* 0.25 km – *c.* 35 km), the monuments are represented by a node on the perimeter of a circle, each visual link by a connecting arc, and the direction of each link (from-to) by a directional arrow. This constructs the visual framework.

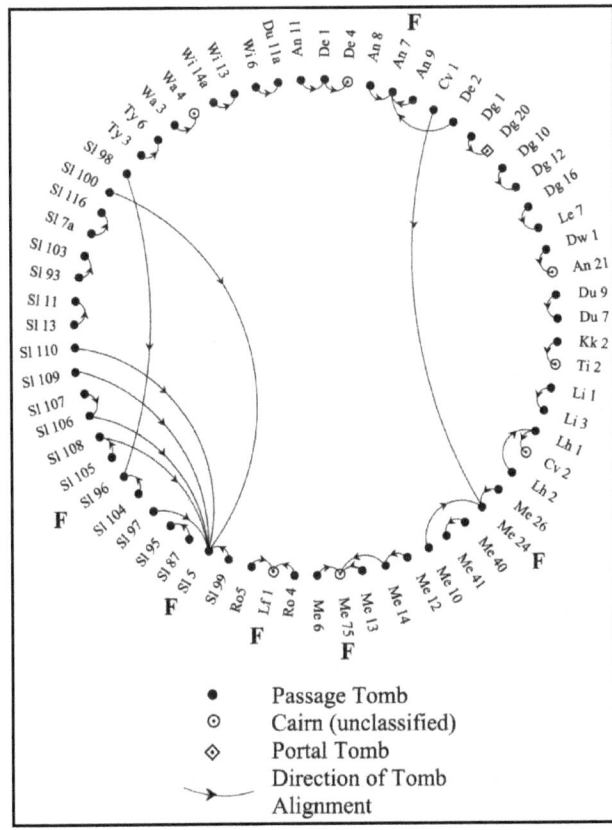

Fig. 1.5. Scale-free visual framework of linked passage tombs and cairns.

Instances of multiple intervisibility are evident, and potentially new focal tombs and cairns (F) identified. There are no examples of tombs being reciprocally aligned. This could have important chronological significance relating to the sequence of tomb building in Ireland, and have cultural questions and interpretations relevant to the debate on the Neolithic embedded within this data.

Hilltop cairns

Tomb alignment towards hilltop cairns occurs in seven instances (see Table 1.1, col.8, classification C; also Figure 1.5). Within that group, the evidence also indicates that the cairns on Kingstown & Carnuff (Me75) and Cornhill (Lf1) are aligned on by three of the passage tombs at Loughcrew, and by the two passage tombs at Sheegeragh, respectively. This raises the possibility that all seven cairns could be culturally and symbolically linked to the passage tomb tradition, making them candidate sites for further archaeological investigation and potential reclassification. It is both interesting and cautionary to note however, that cairns in general can be interpreted as having a wide variety of meaning and chronology. Modern cairns continue to be created by hill climbers and existing ones of unknown antiquity are added to, sometimes continuing an unbroken, unexplainable and compulsive universal human tradition.

DISCUSSION

Any discussion on monument positioning, alignment and meaning is best approached with the awareness that any number of factors - cultural, environmental, psychological and cosmological - could have provided the motivation for those who constructed the passage tombs and cairns. To approach such a discussion from a limited, narrow or untested perspective could incur what in statistics is termed a TYPE I or TYPE II error - reporting a positive effect when there is none (a false positive) *i.e.* the error of accepting an alternative hypothesis of interest when the alignments (for example) could be attributed to chance: or reporting a null effect when there is one (a false negative) *i.e.* the error of failing to observe a difference or an anomaly in what occurs naturally or randomly, such as an intent by the builders in (say) deliberately aligning certain tombs for culturally specific imperatives. Such logic and controls are advisedly extended to any consideration of relevant archaeological data such as that presented in this paper, in order to avoid the risks of misinterpreting the data, and proposing misleading, biased or erroneous interpretations, and derived contexts.

Hypothesis testing of the five alignment distributions presented in Figure 1.3 will be undertaken by the author, but not until the data in the largest distribution (Category 4) can be further investigated for possible sub-distributions. Only then may any reliable and meaningful conclusions, interpretations and cultural contexts be offered. Pending that research and analysis, what is immediately apparent is the anomalously large and unexpected number of passage tombs in Category 1 i.e. those aligned on tombs or cairns. While one is inclined not to pre-empt the results of further statistical and other analyses, it may be useful at this juncture, to make preliminary comments on the possible symbolism and meaning inherent in the apparent pattern discovered in the tomb alignments, and with reference to the horizontal and vertical reference planes.

Symbolic Height

In an attempt to explore the possible phenomenological significances of the data above, we might usefully look to more recently constructed examples of monumentality and meaning undertaken in Ireland.

For the design of the 120 metre high Millennium Spire in Dublin (currently the world's tallest work of art), its architect was keen to learn from the lessons of recent history. The ideology behind the erection of statues to dead heroes for example, instead of inspiring the living as was intended, becomes lost from a world below that is more concerned with the present. The hero may look down on busy passers-by but the latter will rarely reciprocate. Thus importantly, he states:

> [The Spire is not a monument to an individual; nor to a famous poet or soldier. Nor is it a monument to the past. It is a monument to Ireland's contemporary condition and the nation's future in the third millennium. This forward-looking aspiration challenges the usual historical expectations of a monument.]
>
> Ian Ritchie, 2004

Yet Ritchie also recognises the tradition of the passage tomb builders by echoing the symbolism of their spiral decoration engraved on the entrance kerb stone (K1) at Newgrange through his logarithmic (*sic*) spiral in the horizontal bronze base of this iconic monument.

From the perspective of the established church in Ireland, towers and steeples represented authority during the 18th century. For any other religion to erect such a structure was tantamount to an affront and was thus prohibited in an Act passed by the British House of Commons in 1791 (Grimes, 2005: 285-287). By the time Irish Catholic churches were permitted in the mid-nineteenth century, spires and steeples of this religion rapidly began to eclipse those of the established church.

These two examples provide a classic contemporary and a historical example of the power, symbolism and phenomenology of tall and sacred or secular structures, and their capacity to be imbued with cultural identity and meaning over an extended domain, by virtue of their height and visibility. Therein lies the inspiration and motivation to conquer the vertical domain, realised through the link between the human psyche and action.

The Height of Archaeology - Archaeology in Height?

As anyone who has climbed even a modest hill will attest, it is not the absolute height above sea level that is significant. Rather, it is the gradient of the ascent and resulting rapidity with which the climber acquires a commanding view of the world below and the surrounding landscape beyond. From a height, one is removed both physically and psychologically from the concerns and turmoil of daily life, to be replaced with contemplative gain (Tuan, 1993). Furthermore, and as the climber achieves ever greater height separation from 'below', a sense of spirituality becomes apparent, in proportion to the increase in vertical height. Proximity to the infinity of 'space' induces new emotions and fears. And when there is cloud to provide a virtual ceiling and reference above, the sense of approaching a 'world boundary' is very apparent. Such a multi-sensory experience can also produce feelings of power over the surrounding visible domain. It is thus reasonable to argue that such emotions would have provided the psychological impetus to select such places and spaces to locate and build the passage tombs and cairns. Whereas today, we climb for the aesthetic experience, it is probable that in prehistoric times, people may have perceived certain mountains and hills as places only to be ventured onto at certain times of year, and for specific tasks and acts, as sanctioned by the group or society leaders in accordance with prevailing cultural practices and traditions. The summits would have been perceived as being closer to the apparent dome of the celestial sphere - a secondary world about which prehistoric peoples could have had little comprehension of the reality that we now fully understand. The ontological question of 'what is out there' in relation to their perceptions of the celestial sphere and their aspirations to build specific tombs closest to it, therefore touches philosophy, cosmology and psychology.

The phenomenon of tomb alignment towards higher structures and places could therefore be explained within such a psychological and hierarchical framework.

The act of locating tombs on hills and mountains can readily be associated with various symbolic associations and meanings in many cultures. For a tomb located on a summit, it may have been afforded a primacy synonymous with that of the mountain itself and the heavens above, and become more symbolic than the tombs below, as a result. Its consequential 360° view (this aspect will be the subject of more research) could be seen as drawing additional symbolic power from the surrounding landscape and communities. Tombs located below the summit but orientated towards the higher summit or focal tomb (looking up), might be regarded as hierarchically inferior but nonetheless positively and symbolically linked. Interestingly, in Chinese culture, the act of climbing a mountain is regarded as a positive act, but undertaken by the 'inferior' person located in the realm of the 'superior'. Though separated in time and place, the meaning and motivation for the apparent 'positive' relationship overwhelmingly evident in the high positioning and alignment of many of the Irish passage tombs (Table 1.1) may have a shared inheritance and unchanged relevance with our modern world-view.

CONCLUSIONS

The fieldwork and data presented in this paper form part of continuing doctoral research on Irish passage tombs. Although initially daunted by the magnitude of the task, what initially seemed like an over-ambitious and extended study area has yielded new data and findings, with the potential to additionally inform our understanding and perspectives on the meaning and motivation for passage tomb construction.

Any concerns or inherent limitations that might arise in this study by the exclusion of similar enquiries relating to the other categories of tomb, may well prove to be redressed and offset by the breadth and primacy of the data set, and the more secure conclusions to be thus gained from a consideration of the entire *corpus* of Irish passage tombs. Already, this has revealed potentially new patterns of alignment and linking between sites that were not previously known. In addition, the solar astronomical potential at sites where passages are extant, observed horizon data, and measures of visibility between tombs will be the subject of additional analysis hopefully leading to new interpretations and relevance.

Preliminary indications from this research suggest that the complex symbolisms inherent in the passage tomb culture, which are more obviously expressed in tomb morphology, material culture, art and tomb clustering for example, may also extend into the spatial relationships evidently inherent in this homogenous group of monuments. This could be indicative of new and different cultural imperatives and meaning, and have the potential and relevance to better inform our understanding of the Neolithic at the wider regional level as well as at local level.

Acknowledgements

Dr. Muiris O'Sullivan and Professor Gabriel Cooney, School of Archaeology, University College Dublin for supervision and guidance. Professor Tadhg O'Keeffe of UCD, for the stimulus and learning received at innumerable post-graduate seminars. Professor Tom Ray, Dublin Institute for Advanced Studies, for participation in fieldwork at Loughcrew. Kevin Mooney and Alain Chenaux, Dublin Institute of Technology for constructive comments. Paula Prendergast for logistical support with field work.

This project is funded by the Dublin Institute of Technology.

References

BERG, S. (1995) - Landscape of the Monuments: A study of the passage tombs in the Cúil Iarra region, Co. Sligo, Ireland. Stockholm: Riksantikvarieämbetet Arkeologiska undersökningar. 256 p.

BURENHULT, G. (1984) - The Archaeology of Carrowmore: Environmental Archaeology and the Megalithic Tradition at Carrowmore, Co. Sligo, Ireland. Theses and Papers in North-European Archaeology. Stockholm. 14.

BURENHULT, G. (1988) - The Swedish Archaeological Excavations at Carrowmore, Co.Sligo, Ireland. [Consult. 20 October 2005]. Available on www_URL: http:/www.hgo.se/Carrowmore. 28 p.

CODY, E. (2002) - Survey of the Megalithic Tombs of Ireland, Volume VI: County Donegal. Bray: Wordwell. 298 p.

COONEY, G. (1990) - The place of megalithic tomb cemeteries in Ireland. Antiquity York. 64, p. 741-53.

COONEY, G. (2000) - Landscapes of Neolithic Ireland. London: Routledge. 276 p.

COONEY, G.; GROGAN, E. (1998) - People and Place during the Irish Neolithic: Exploring Social Change in Time and Place. In EDMONDS, M.; RICHARDS, C., eds - Understanding the Neolithic of north-western Europe. Glasgow: Cruithne Press, p. 457-480.

COONEY, G.; GROGAN, E. (1999) - Irish Prehistory. Dublin: Wordwell. 276 p.

CORLETT, C. (1994) - The Origins of Megalithic Tombs in Atlantic Europe. Trowel VI: University College Dublin: Archaeological Society, p. 12-17.

DE VALERA, R. (1959-60) - The Court Cairns of Ireland. Proceedings of the Royal Irish Academy (C) Dublin. 60, p. 9-140.

DESCARTES, R (1628) - Regulae ad directionem Ingenii. In KEMP, N., Descartes Philosophical Writings (1958). New York: Random House. 316 p.

EOGAN, G. (c. 1986) - Knowth and the Passage Tombs of Ireland. London: Thames and Hudson. 247 p.

EOGAN, G.; ROCHE, H. (1997) - Excavations at Knowth 2 : Settlement and Ritual Rites of the Fourth and Third Millennia BC. Dublin: Royal Irish Academy. 311 p.

FRASER, S. (1998) - The Public Forum and the Space Between: the Materiality of Social Strategy in the Irish Neolithic. Proceedings of the Prehistoric Society. Cambridge. 64, p. 203-24.

GRIMES, B. (2005) - The architecture of Dublin's neo-classical Roman Catholic temples 1803-1862. (Unpublished PhD thesis). Dublin: National College of Art and Design.

HERITY, M. (1974) - Irish Passage Graves. Dublin: Irish University Press. 308 p.

HOUSTON, S.; TAUBE, K. (2000) - An Archaeology of the Senses: Perception and Cultural Expression in Ancient Mesoamerica. Cambridge Archaeological Journal. Cambridge. 10: 2, p. 261-294.

KILFEATHER, A. (1997) - A Tomb with a View (Unpublished PhD thesis). University of Reading.

McGUINNESS, D. (1995) - The Passage Tombs of County Dublin. Trowel VI. Dublin: University College Dublin/ Archaeological Society, p. 5-11.

MCMANN, J. (1994) - Forms of Power: dimensions of an Irish Landscape. Antiquity York. 68, p. 525-44.

Ó NUALLÁIN, S. (1983) - Irish Portal Tombs: topography, siting and distribution. Proceedings of the Royal Irish Academy (C). Dublin. 113, p. 75-105.

Ó NUALLÁIN, S. (1989) - Survey of the Megalithic Tombs of Ireland, Volume V: County Sligo. Dublin: Stationary Office.

O'SULLIVAN, M. (1997) - On the Meaning of Megalithic Art. Brigantium. La Coruña.10, p. 23-35.

O'SULLIVAN, M. (2005) - The Mound of the Hostages. Bray: Wordwell. 334 p.

PRENDERGAST, F. (Forthcoming) - Visual Signatures in the Irish Neolithic landscape: a wider perspective on the Irish passage tombs. In BELMONTE, J.; ZEDDA, M. eds.- Proceedings of the thirteenth SEAC Conference, Isili, Sardinia, June 28th-July 3rd 2005.

RITCHIE, I. (2004) - The Spire. Herne Bay: Categorical Books. 96 p.

RUGGLES, C. (1999) - Astronomy in Prehistoric Britain and Ireland. New Haven, Conn., London: Yale University Press. 285 p.

SHEE-TWOHIG, E. (2004) - Irish Megalithic Tombs (2nd ed.). Princes Risborough: Shire Books. 72 p.

STOUT, G. (1994) - Wicklow's Prehistoric Landscape. In HANNIGAN, G.; NOLAN, W., eds - Wicklow: History and Society. Dublin: Geography Publications, p. 1-40.

SMARDON, R. [et al., eds] (1986) - Foundations for Visual Project Analysis. New York: Wiley. 374 p.

TEDLOCK, D. (1996) - Popul Vuh: the Definitive Edition of the Mayan Book of the Dawn of Life and the Glories of Gods and Kings. New York: Simon and Schuster.

TUAN, Y-F. (1993) - Passing Strange and Wonderful. Washington, DC: Island Press. 288 p.

TILLEY, C. (1994) - A Phenomenology of Landscape. Oxford: Berg. 221 p.

ZUBE, E. (1986) - Landscape values: history, concepts, and applications. In SMARDON, R.; PALMER, J.; FELLEMAN, J., eds - Foundations for Visual Project Analysis. New York: Wiley, p. 3-19.

CELESTIAL SYMBOLS ON BRONZE AGE ARCHAEOLOGICAL FINDS IN THE CARPATHIAN BASIN – CASE STUDY

Emília PÁSZTOR

Matrica Museum, Hungary, pasztore@enternet.hu

Abstract: Cognitive archaeology has become a fashionable but necessary field for searching new methods of reconstructing the past. For prehistoric societies when there is little factual background, one must be very cautious and apply as many means that can be found in available material as possible in order not to create science fictional ideas. In this case study the author wants to examine the possibility of investigating solar cult on the base of decorated objects and orientation of graves in two late Bronze Age cemeteries of the Carpathian Basin.
Keywords: Carpathian Basin, Late Bronze Age, cemetery, orientation, solar symbols.

Résumé: L' Archeologie Cognitive est devenue une mode mais un champ necessaire pour la recherche de nouveaux methodes de la reconstruction du passé. Pour les societées prehistoriques, quand il-y-a peu d' information factuelle, on doit être très prudent et appliquer tous les moyens qu' on peut trouver dans les matériaux disponibles de façon à créer des idées scientifiques fictionnelles. Dans cet étude, l' auteur veut examiner la possibilitée de rechercher le culte solaire basée dans les objects décorés et l' orientation des sépultures dans deux cimetières du Bronze Final du Bassin des Carpathes.
Mots clés: Bassin des Carpathes, Bronze Final, cimetière, orientation, symboles solaires.

> "When we see cosmology derived solely from the alleged orientation of a building to a particular star, when we see an entire ideology reconstructed from the style of a carving, and when we see ancient religion reconstructed from a handful of figurines, we have a right to be skeptical."
>
> (Flannery *et al.1998:*46).

INTRODUCTION

Study of 'iconography' by archaeologists means investigating how ancient people represented their ideological, political, religious and or cosmological ideas in their art. In non-literate societies where history or ethnohistory cannot support the analysis, it is very difficult to avoid involving the authors' personality. Iconography should and can work sufficiently when it is analytical and draws on as wide a range of social and natural sciences as it is possible (Flannery *et al.* 1998: 43-45).

Although written sources are not fundamental for cognitive archaeology new ideas are difficult to prove without them, despite the fact that they can also provide false information. The analyses of visual representation on artefacts are essential, however, it is often difficult to decide whether the decorations were applied intentionally and involved a shared knowledge with the whole community or they were only interactions (Renfrew *et al.* 2004: 394-402).

There is good evidence that solar and lunar phenomena played a particularly important role in Bronze Age mythology in Europe. During this period the increasing use of special symbols assumed to be solar is well known and easily discernible on different types of archaeological artefacts. Essays on prehistoric mythology frequently mention the evident existence of lunar or especially solar cults (Green, 1993; Kristiansen *et al.* 2006). Yet, they invariably repeat a well known list of examples of artefacts and rock art from many different parts of Europe. Yet there is hardly anybody who has ever made a detailed, integrated investigation of tombs, artefacts, and other relevant archaeological evidence in a particular area in the Bronze Age. Fleming Kaul belongs to the few exceptions. Devoting important role to the sun he developed basement for Scandinavian Bronze Age religion by making a detailed study of depictions on bronze razors from the Late Bronze Age (Kaul 2004). Turning to the other parts of prehistoric Europe, are there any proof of a general solar cult in the Bronze Age?

CULT ACTIVITIES INCLUDED INFLUENCE OF CELESTIAL PHENOMENA IN THE CARPATHIAN BASIN

The early finds in the Carpathian Basin, in particular, have hardly been systematically examined with regard to the concepts in the chapter title. The sun as a protective symbol or the part of complex, likely regeneration symbols was only mentioned by some authors (Sági, 1976; Schreiber, 1984). There is an imperative need for innovative methods in order to obtain genuine results and for not making the same mistakes as criticized above. At the very beginnings, however, one should be aware of that some beautiful solar symbols do not necessarily make a solar cult and 'sun' symbols might have been pure decorations or at the most a protective sign. As for the possible celestial symbols on artifacts, several questions can be raised when developing the research:

- Were these sun-like decorations real astral/sun symbols belonging to a certain archaeological culture, or were they so generally used that their origin cannot be followed back?
- Could they symbolize a genuine sun or moon cult, id est. a particular activity involving ritual practices that may be reflected in other aspects of the material culture such as the orientation of graves or tombs, sanctuaries, or shrines;

Generally it is not possible to decipher or rather interpret the meaning of a symbol explicitly from the symbolical depiction of an object or a picture. What matters is the whole assemblage and not the single finds taken out of their context.

Keeping this principle in mind and even developing it for the Carpathian Basin where there are no remains of prehistoric monuments of raised stones above the ground, the following methodical approach for a complex research of the Bronze Age have been set up:

Orientations of graves and their possible relations to grave goods

Special arrangements of goods in tombs or graves

Frequency of celestial symbols on grave artefacts

Orientations of houses

Many archaeologists consider the prevailing wind as almost exclusive reason for orientations of houses. They have a tendency not to take into consideration any other possible interpretations, although the ethno-historical investigations have long argued the important role of non-environmental factors in creating a home to live in. A survey of comparison between the orientations of the Linear Pottery Culture houses and the prevailing winds has been made in different regions of Central Europe. The result showed there was certainly a link between the house orientation and prevailing summer winds but this did not apply to all the areas occupied by Danubian groups (Coudart, 1998: 84-89).

Orientations of 'cult' structures

This is the weakest part of the complex investigation of the cultural groups of Bronze Age as hardly any structures, which might belong to cultic remains, have been excavated in the Carpathian Basin.

There is high number of investigations dealing with orientations of prehistoric monuments in whole Europe, although most of them refer to megalithic remains (Ruggles, 1999). The results show a clear picture: orientation of a single building/structure is not convincing enough, and what is more important is the orientations solely rarely furnish the possible solar or moon cult with solid proof. The initial case studies relating to orientation of Early and Late Bronze Age houses and solar symbols on artefacts belonging the Bell Beaker Csepel group of the Carpathian Basin are very promising as they seem to support an important role of the sun in the beliefs (Pásztor, 2006, 2005; Endrődi *et al.* 2006).

'Celestial' symbols on archaeological finds

Investigating the elements of decorations on archaeological finds, the most difficult part is to decide whether the symbol can be included among the celestial symbols or not. A complex assemblage of motives or patterns or rather a whole picture containing the sign under discussion can help with drawing conclusions. The decorations on Bronze Age finds from the Carpathian Basin, however, are quite abstract and impede the work rather than support it. The sun, moon and star signs are most easily recognisable when they are like child drawings – a circle with rays, a crescent or just crossing rays, although only few artefacts can be listed with confidence as sun, moon and stars.

By looking at representation of the sun on archaeological finds of the Carpathian Basin, especially on precious objects, the symbols assumed solar are always richly decorated with concentric circles and spirals and can display radial rays (Neugebauer, 1987: Abb 51, 54; Kovács, 1999; 1991) (Fig 2.1). The more simple circles are often also believed to be the sun (Endrödi *et al*, 2006), as the example of Nebra disc might prove (Schlosser, 2002; Meller, 2002; Pásztor *et al*, 2007), although they might actually have been of the full moon.

Unfortunately, the portrayal of the lunar crescent is almost completely missing on decorations in the Carpathian Basin, although it is rendered in ending parts of precious golden arm rings and armlets (Kovács, 1999: Figs. 26, 27). It is natural for the stars displaying radiating ray pattern that is so distinctive when looking at bright stars (Navarro *et al.*, 1997) and this seems to be a characteristic feature for star symbols on other objects from the first part of the Bronze Age in the Carpathian Basin as well, although these symbols are difficult to distinguish from sun symbols (Koós, 1988: 1.kep; Kovacs, 1991: Abb.2, Abb. 5).

Simple circles can also stand for stars as it might be the case with the Nebra disc (Pásztor *et al.* 2007) and some representations on rock carvings. Depicting the stars as round objects might have been intentional. In ethnographical reports on cosmological beliefs of people in the northern part of Eurasia and North America, the stars are imagined as holes in the sky (MacDonald, 2000: 33). The Pleiades were also called Szitáslyuk or A sieve with holes in old Hungarian language, which is supposed to be of ancient Finno-Ugric origin (Zsigmond, 1999: 48).

There might have been a special connection between a celestial phenomenon and its colour on painted artefacts.

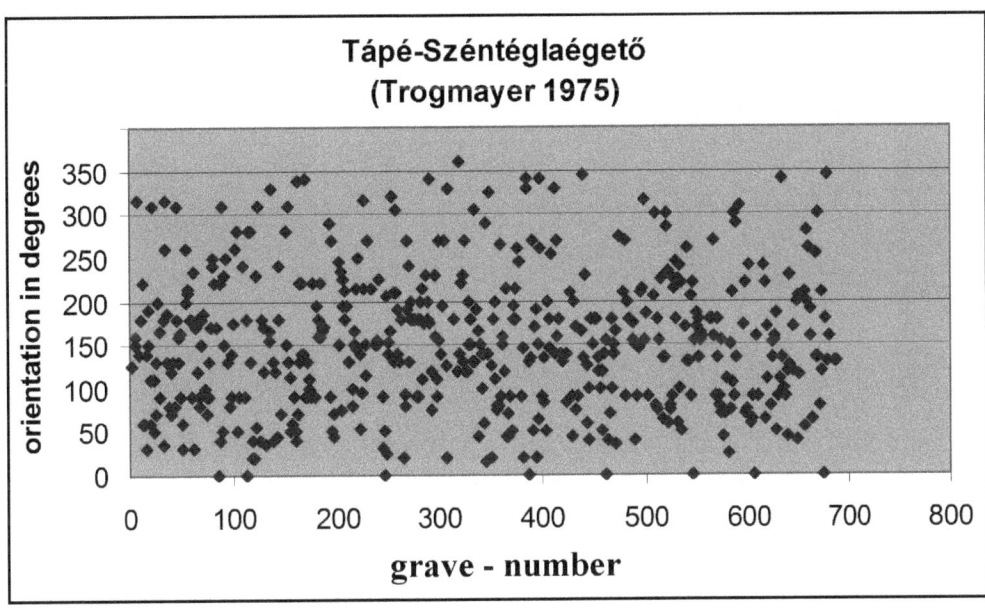

Figure 2.1. The orientation of the graves at Tápé – Széntéglaégető, Hungary.

We have some knowledge of the intentional use of special colours in ceremonies, and of the perceived colour of the sun and the moon.

BURIAL RITE AND THE SUN

During the case study it was assumed that different communities represented by the cemeteries shared a same belief system about the Otherworld as they belonged to the same archaeological cultural group. The reflection of these common beliefs in material culture related to burial rite was expected to be rather similar. When they buried their dead relatives and furnished the graves with goods, their acts were partly guided by the shared symbolical awareness.

Cemeteries of the Late Bronze Age Tumulus Culture

At the beginning of the Late Bronze Age, not only new economic and politic changes but new incomers are also supposed to enter the Carpathian Basin from the west. The material remains of the new archaeological culture seem to be related most to the archaeological finds of the West-Central European Tumulus culture, thus the same name was applied for the new material culture. Their heritage has been discovered mostly in cemeteries in the Carpathian Basin. The grave goods despite of the above mentioned relation, however significantly differ from those of South Germany, Bohemia and Austria. There are differences in the proportion of bi-ritual burial ceremonies on different areas. All these support the assumption that the descendants of local Middle Bronze Age inhabitants also participated in creating the changes.

The cemeteries in the Carpathian Basin contain inhumations and cremations as well. The two types of burial custom co-existed with each other and applied in the same cemetery. Cremation even occurred in the home land of the culture, in South Germany and Austria, although the inhumation was dominant. The proportion of applying cremation generally increased in the cemeteries of the Carpathian Basin, although the custom of the local inhabitants must have had a great influence on its actual ratio of a site. The deceased were buried or placed on funeral pyre with their bronze or sometimes golden jewels and arms. Ceramic vessels containing food were also placed into the graves. The urns were generally covered by bowls. The decoration style and the shape of the ceramics in the graves often show connection with the local craft heritage (Csányi, 2003: 161-163).

The cemeteries at the site of Tápé and Tiszafüred have been chosen for case study as like the ones of Jánoshida and Etyek, as well as Salka in Slovakia have high number of graves and are mostly contemporary.

Tápé-Szénteglaégető

The site situated in Csongrád County, the South of Hungary. The cemetery was excavated and published by Otto Trogmayer (Trogmayer, 1975). 686 graves were unearthed. 517 graves contained skeleton, 37 graves had ashes and the burial rite of 132 graves cannot be identified. The considerable part of inhumation can be assigned to the influence of the earlier local Perjamos culture whose burial rite involved inhumation.

The excavator measured the orientation of the graves and where it was possible that of the skeletons, the differences between them were very small. The chart (Figure 2.1) shows the orientations of graves with registered numbers for the whole cemetery.

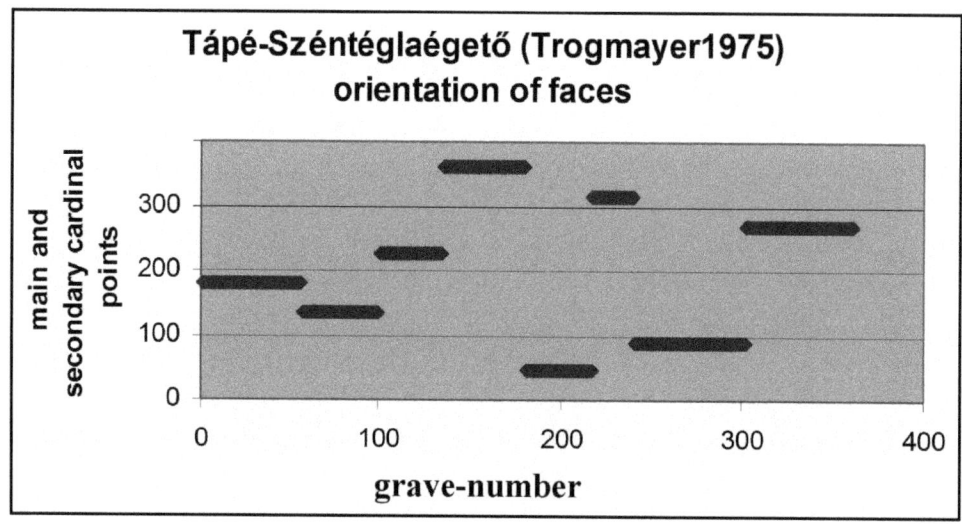

Figure 2.2. The orientation of faces of skeleton at site Tápé- Széntéglaégető, Hungary.

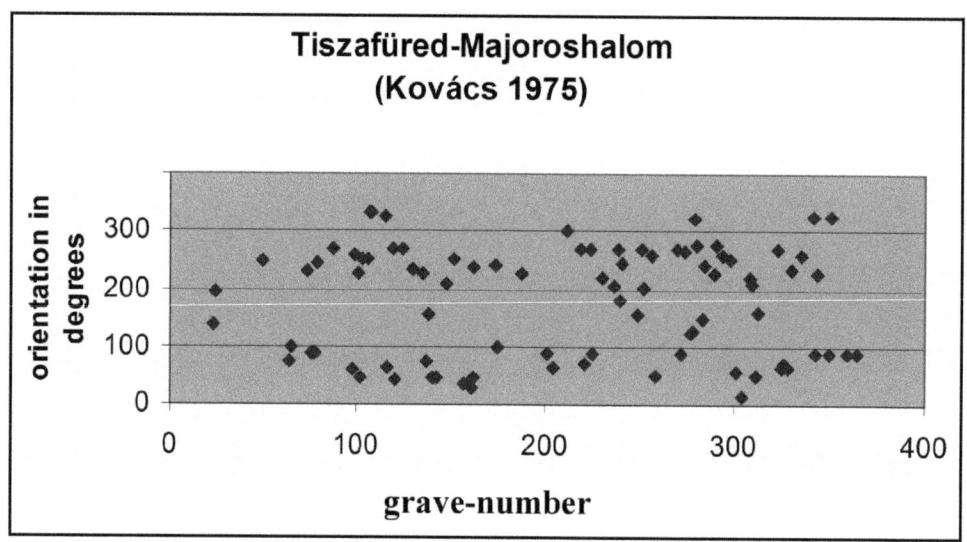

Figure 2.3. The orientations of the graves at site Tiszafüred – Majoroshalom, Hungary.

As it can be seen on the chart no significance in orientation can be detected for the 517 graves of the Tumulus culture, although 75% of the graves were orientated. No correlations can be shown separately for men, children, furnished graves or graves with contracted skeleton on the left side or right side either. The same can be said when the orientation plotted against the directions of faces (Figure 2.2)

10 graves of 360 inhumation and 3 of 37 cremation graves furnished with goods contained ceramics with sun symbols (Table 2.1). This proportion is so low that we can argue neither the orientation nor the symbols on finds support the presence of the sun in the burial rite at this site.

Tiszafüred – Majoroshalom

The site is situated in Szolnok County, East of Hungary. The cemetery was excavated and published by Tibor Kovács (Kovács, 1975). 365 graves was unearthed. 132 graves contained skeletons, 111 had cremation and in 112 the burial rite cannot be identified. The significant proportion of the inhumation as burial rite must have been the result of the strong connection with the local Füzesabony culture. This culture, which flourished in Middle Bronze Age buried their deceased with strict orientation, South – North for males and North-South for females in contracted position. It was not till the late phase of the Füzesabony culture called Bodrogszerdahely when some graves with ashes strewn on the floor of the grave pits were discovered. Since then the rules for orientations might have relaxed as from 10 to 20 degrees of deviation from the North-South line can be measured.

The chart shows the orientation of the whole cemetery with inhumation graves (Figure 2.3). Although 132 graves belonged to this rite, but orientation in degrees could be measured only for 89.

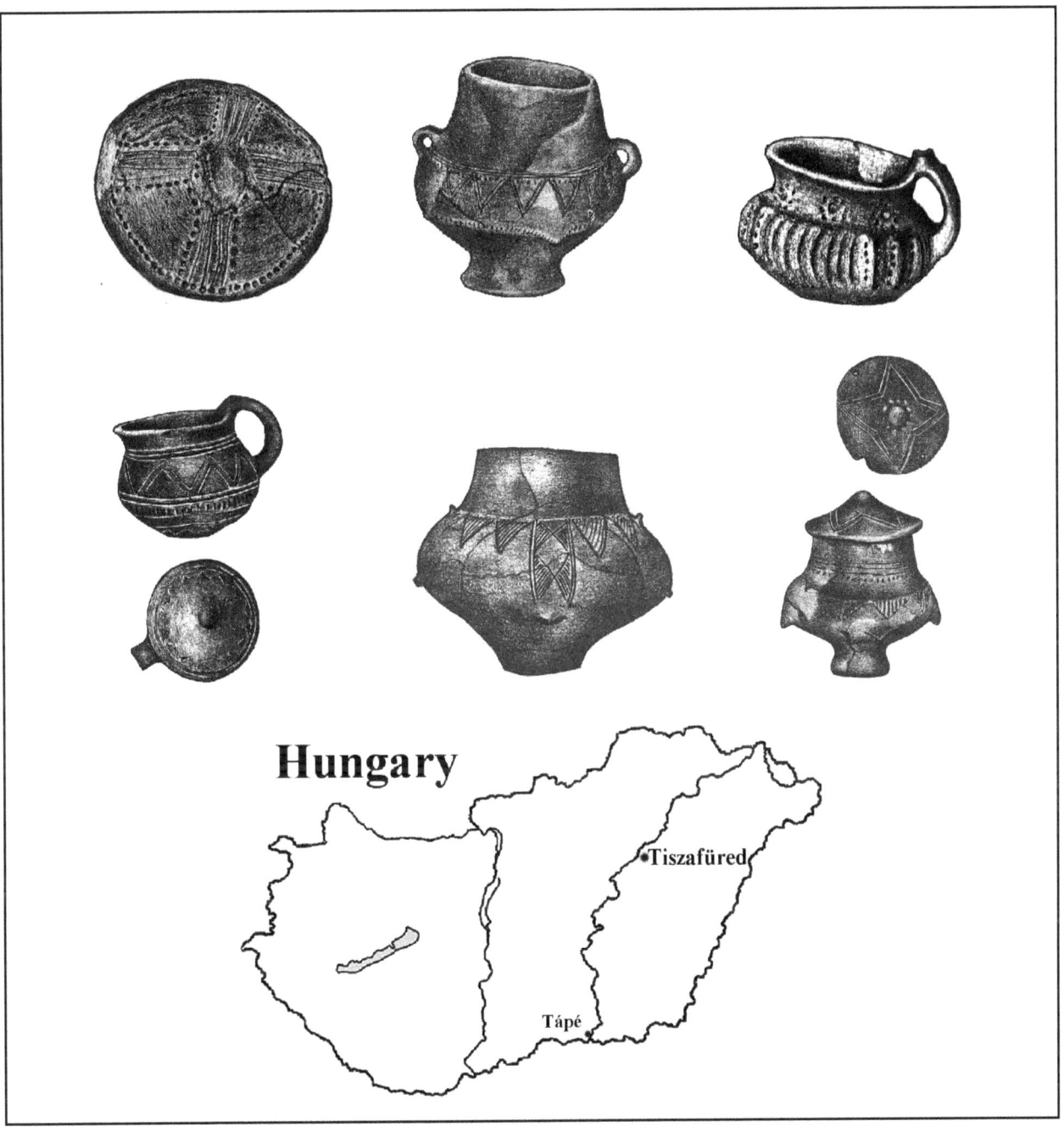

Table 2.1. Different types of vessels with solar or astral decorations
from the Tumulus culture cemetery of Tápé- Széntéglaégető, Hungary.

It can be seen on the chart that there is some concentration around East and West. Let's suppose that East-West orientation of a grave (pit) was worked out in the morning or in the afternoon around the burial day and they used the actual sunrise or sunset as a reference for this activity. The chart on Figure 2.4 shows those graves whose orientations are between ± 36° from the East-West line. These values approximately show the northernmost and southernmost sunrise in the Bronze Age in the Carpathian Basin. The concentration around the East-West line can be seen more clearly, consequently 51 graves of 89, i.e. 57% might have been oriented to the sunrise or sunset (of the burial day).

If the graves with finds showing local heritage or influence are plotted against their orientations, the following chart can be seen (Figure 2.5).

This chart shows some concentration around the North – South line, as it would be expected for the graves with some heritage of the Füzesabony culture, although the deviation from the North-South line is quite high, about 50°.

12 graves of 132 inhumations and 52 graves of 111 cremations contained finds decorated with solar symbols (Table 2.2). The proportion for inhumation graves is low

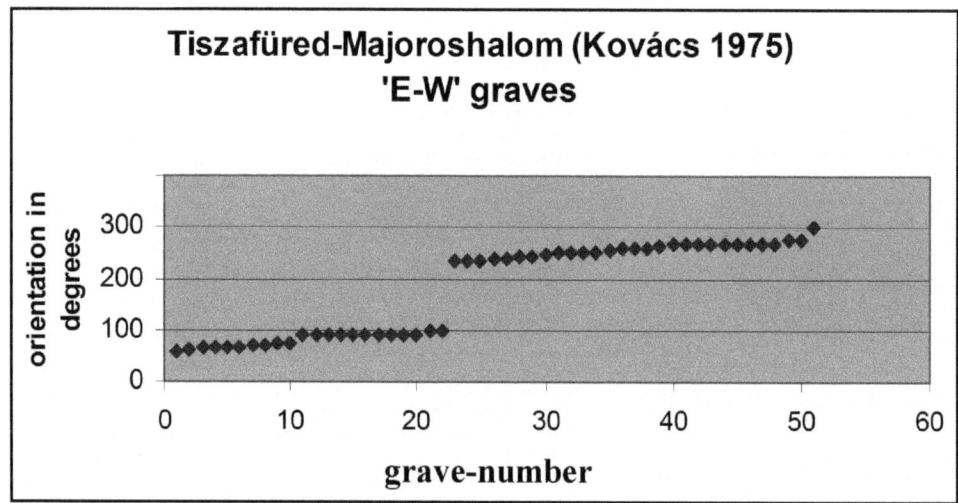

Figure 2.4. The orientations of graves to the sunrise or sunset of the burial day.

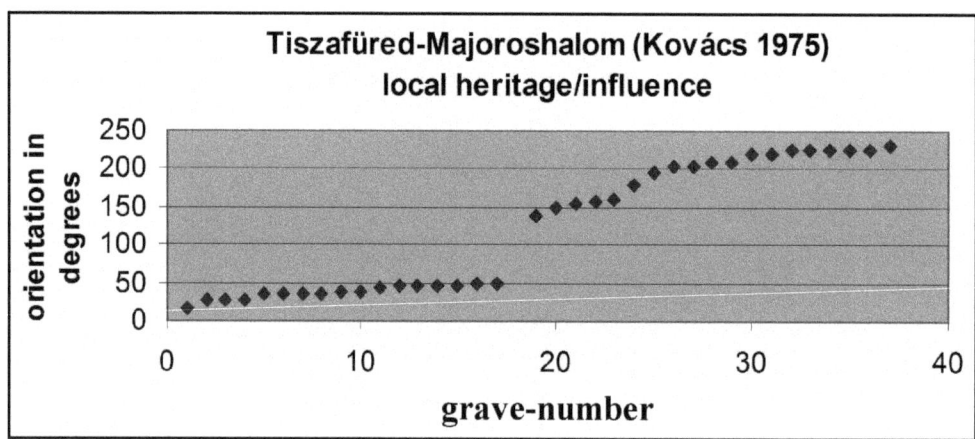

Figure 2.5. The orientations of graves with goods showing local influence.

but it is not the case for the cremation graves. This high rate of 47% might be assigned to the symbolical relation between the sun and the fire of burial pyre.

CONCLUSIONS DRAWN FROM THIS CASE STUDY

- Different sites of an archaeological culture can show different degrees of using sun symbols,
- There might not have been common principles for cult activities in burial rite even inside one culture,
- The influence of contemporary, neighbouring cultural groups can create a 'virtual sun cult',
- To detect the possible impact of sun in ritual life of the Bronze Age, comprehensive investigation of archaeological cultures is needed,

The religious ideas/beliefs cannot always clearly be reflected in material culture. An abstract motif could be used as a pure decoration but as the symbolical attribute of the sun god or goddess. The complex investigations of a culture can explicitly result valuable conclusions and information possible closer the reality.

The archaeologists can work with sufficient success on cognitive topics but only with appropriate rigour in order to avoid fictitious ideas in Bronze Age religion and cosmologies.

References

COUDAR, A. (1998) - *Architecture et société néolithique L'unité et la variance de la maison danubienne*. DAF 67. Paris

CSÁNYI, M. (2003) - Hódítók nyugat felől: a halomsíros kultúra. Visy, Zs. (szerk.), *Magyar régészet az ezredfordulón*. Budapest: NKÖM. p.161-163.

ENDRŐDI, A.; PÁSZTOR, E., (2006) - The role of symbolism and tradition in the society of Bell-Beaker Csepel group. *Archaeológiai Értesítő*. 131, p.7-25.

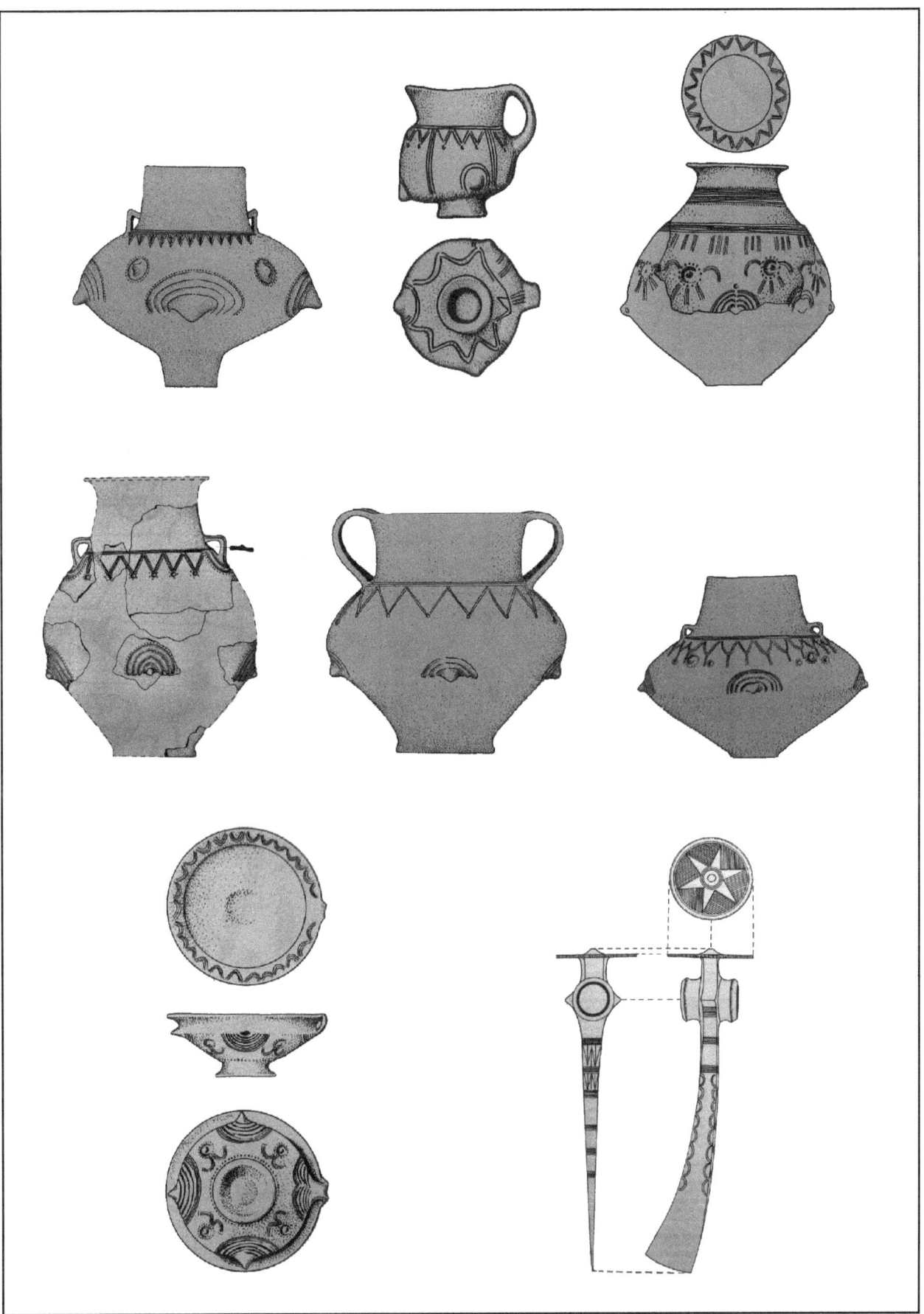

Table 2.2. Different types of vessels and an axe with solar or astral decorations from the Tumulus culture cemetery of Tiszafüred-Majoroshalom, Hungary.

FLANNERY, K. V.; MARCUS, J. (1998) - Cognitive Archaeology in D. S. Whitley (ed). *Reader in Archaeological Theory*. London and New York: Routledge. p.35-48.

GREEN, M. (1993) - The sun gods of ancient Europe. In SINGH, M. (ed.). *The sun, symbols of power and life*. New York: Harry N. Abrams, Inc. p. 295-311.

KAUL, F. (2004) - *Bronzealderens religion*. Coppenhagen: Det Kongellge Nordiske Old Skriftselskab.

KOÓS, J. (1988) - Bronzezeitliches Anhängsel von Nagyrozvágy. *HOMÉ*. 25-26, p. 69-80.

KOVÁCS, T. (1999) - Bronzezeit. In KOVÁCS, T.; RACZKY, P. (eds) *Prähistorische Goldschatze aus dem ungarischem Nationalmuseum*. Budapest: MNM/Elte-Régészettudományi Intézet, p. 37-63.

KOVÁCS, T. (1991) - Das bronzezeitliche Goldarmband Von Dunavecse, *Folia Archaeologica*. 42, p. 7-25.

KOVÁCS, T. (1974) - *Tumulus culture cemeteries of Tiszafüred*. Budapest: MNM

KRISTIANSEN, K.; LARSSON, T. B. (2005) - *The rise of Bronze Age society*. Cambridge University Press.

MACDONALD, J. (2000) - *The arctic sky*. Iqaluit: Nunavut Research Institute.

MELLER, H. (2002) - Die Himmelscheibe von Nebra – ein Frühbronzezeitliche Fund von aussergewöhnlicher Bedeutung. *Archäologie in Sachen-Anhalt*. Band 1, p. 7-20.

NAVARRO, R.; LOSADA, M.A. (1997) - Shape of stars and optical quality of the human eye. *Journal of the Optical Society of America*. A 14, p. 353-359.

NEUGEBAUER, J.W. (1987) - *Die Bronzezeit im Osten Österreichs*. St. Pölten – Wien: NP Verlag.

PÁSZTOR, E. (2006) - The Connection between the Terrestrial and Celestial Landscape during the Bronze Age in the Carpathian Basin: Orientation of houses. Presented at EAA conference, Cracow 2006: EAA conference book /BAR International Series. in press.

PÁSZTOR, E. (2005) - Sunshine in Bell Beaker's houses: On the Orientation of the Houses of the Bell Beaker - Csepel Group. SEAC conference book. in press.

PÁSZTOR, E.; ROSLUND, C. (2007) - The interprettation of the Nebra Disc. *Antiquit* 81: 267-78.

RENFREW, C.; BAHN, P. (2004) - *Archaeology: theories, methods and practice*. London: Thames and Hudson.

RUGGLES, C. L. N. (1999) - *Astronomy in Prehistoric Britain and Ireland*. New Haven/London: Yale University Press.

SÁGI, K. (1976) - Árpád-kori varázslás régészeti emlékei. VMMK 6, p. 55-85.

SCHLOSSER, W. (2002) - Zur astronomischen Deutung der Himmelsscheibe von Nebra. *Archäologie in Sachen-Anhalt*. Band 1, p. 21-23.

SCHREIBER, R. (1984) - Szimbólikus ábrázolások korabronzkori edényeken (Symbolic depictions on Early Bronze Age vessels). *Archaeologiai Értesítő* 111. p. 3-28.

TROGMAYER, O. (1975) - *Das Bronzezeitliche Graberfeld bei Tápé. Fontes Archaeologici Hungariae*. Budapest: Akadémia Kiadó.

ZSIGMOND, GY. (1999) - *Égitest és néphagyomány* ('Celestial objects and folk heritage' summary in English). Csikszereda: Pallas-Akadémia Könyvkiadó.

THE "DOMESTICATION" OF THE WORLD INTO A HOUSE AND A HOME: COSMOGRAPHIC SYMBOLISM AS A BASIC EXPRESSION OF THE HUMAN MIND

Michael A. RAPPENGLÜCK
University of Munich

Abstract: Cosmographic symbolism seems to be a relevant idea for the interpretation of certain archaeological remains. Evident is a basic human need for organizing the world into a meaningful system of related parts, which helps to integrate and orientate man within an ecosystem. Caves, non-domestic architecture, dwellings (tent, house, temple, tomb), but also a village or a city, and the landscape can serve as cognitive cosmographic models, which permitted man to "domesticate" the unknown world into a known one, his "home". Cosmographic symbolism could be an important field of cognitive and symbolic archaeology.
Keywords: cosmography, landscape, dwelling, cognitive and symbolic archaeology

Résumé: Le symbolisme de cosmographie semble être une idée pertinente pour l'interprétation de certains restes archéologiques. Evident est un besoin humain fondamental pour organiser le monde dans un système significatif de parties apparentées, qui aide à intégrer et orienter l'homme dans l'écosystème. Les cavernes, l'architecture non résidentielle, les habitations (la tente, la maison, le temple, le tombeau), mais aussi un village ou une ville, et le paysage peut servir des modèles cognitifs de cosmographie, qui ont permis l'homme « domestiquer » le monde inconnu comme un monde connu, sa « maison ». Le symbolisme de cosmographie pourrait être un important domaine d'archéologie cognitive et symbolique.
Mots-clés: la cosmographie, le paysage, les habitations, l'archéologie cognitives et symboliques

To begin with, I define the signification of the phrase "cosmographic symbolism": "Cosmographic" denotes a generalized representation of the world, including ideas of its structure (cosmology), its origin (cosmogony), and the relation to human life within, shared and illustrated by the members of a certain social group. "Symbolism" means the way a human community maps mental models into more or less tangible objects and structures, which serve as a kind of well-suited natural and/or artificial information carriers for everyone, who shares the syntax, semantics, and pragmatics of communication, practiced by the community.

Cosmographic symbolism is illustrated by given natural structures and man-made buildings, iconographies, myths, rituals, and of cause written descriptions. The last three are not directly reported by prehistory and only sparsely handed down in protohistory cultures. Thus to get some ideas of cosmographical principles, which could have ideologically influenced and guided human activities in early history, it is necessary to draw attention at the results and approaches in the field of wider science, from cultural anthropology to even primatology. In every case, the very complexity of early cultures makes a fully interdisciplinary research desirable and significant (Rappenglück, 1999: 30-36), which pays attention to the details as much as possible, which is aware of fundamental ambiguities, interactions, and overlapping given in the mind of early man, and which also respects the diversity of today's interpretations. So studying "cosmographic symbolism" could be a very important field of cognitive archaeology, closely related to symbolic archaeology.

Recently David Lewis-Williams in his book "Inside the Neolithic Mind" (Lewis-Williams, 2005) made the technical term "cosmology" interwoven with the so-called neuropsychological model a subject of discussion to understand Palaeolithic and Neolithic mind. Clive Ruggles emphasized and summarized the reflection of cosmological principles in special patterns of the landscape (so-called "sacred geographies") and artificial structures of early history cultures in his study "Astronomy in Prehistoric Britain and Ireland". Ed Krupp presented an overview about "sacred places" starting from Palaeolithic epochs up to historical time in his books "Skywatchers, Shamans & Kings. Astronomy and the Archaeology of Power" (Krupp, 1997) and "Echoes of the Ancient Skies: The Astronomy of Lost Civilizations" (Krupp, 1983). I myself have argued for the existence of a kind of cosmographical symbolism during the Palaeolithic (Rappenglück, 1999, 2005a) and at Lepenski Vir (Rappenglück, 1995) in Neolithic time. The studies above show that there is some evidence for cosmographical symbolism in prehistoric and protohistoric cultures. Nevertheless, how can we recognize and decode it?

What do the archaeological records say? There are evidences of order and orientation patterns concerning the design of prehistoric monuments, such like dwellings, tombs, or the location of special "sacred" places (e.g. rocks, hills, mountains, sources, lakes, rivers, coastline, and caves), the layout of early villages or cities, and the existence of sacred geographies, in which monuments are embedded and related to each other. Examples come from prehistoric and protohistoric cultures worldwide (Barnatt, 1998; Boivin, 2004; Bradley, 2002; Gulløv and Appelt, 2001; Krupp, 1997; Lewis and Stout, 1998; Rappenglück, 1995; Ruggles, 1999). Frequently order and orientation is given by particular "alignments" with focus on one-dimensional sequence and directionality (Ruggles, 1999). In addition one can find domains in which ordering and intensification of certain objects within a special flat space follows a net-like reference system or is done around a centre, often according to an ordinary scale of weighting the arrangement with reference to the middle. Another set of spatial order and orientation is indicated by divisions of a domain along a binary iterated scheme. Furthermore the recognition and ordinary scaling of the third dimension had been a factor of order and orientation. There are examples concerning the importance of vertical arranged strata related to caves, hills, mountains, artificial structures (Lewis-Williams, 2005, Rappenglück, 2005a). Finally there are strong evidences for a time-factored organization of the structures and the landscape (Krupp, 1983: 157-211; 1997: 127-151; Ruggles, 1999). Which clues about cosmographic symbolism can we get further drawing attention to other sciences?

COMMUNICATION WITH COSMIC POWER – FIRE, HEARTH, AND SMOKE OUTLETS

Since Lower Palaeolithic epochs producing and keeping of fire was a very important human activity. Sitting around a fireplace helped to protect against the attacks of wild animals. It was necessary to keep the right distance to the fire to profit from his power and at the same time to avoid burn. This led to a natural domain, in which activities are concentrated an distributed around a fire place. There exist three distances, which define the human intercourse with fire: Looking from the centre to the periphery there is an inner domain where one can put things into the fire for transformation, such as cooking, burning clay, and destruction purposes. Another sphere of activity has its borderline where one isn't able anymore to feel the heat dissipation. Finally the area, where one isn't able to see the light emission defines the outer domain around a fire place. So setting up a fire-place leads to the experience of centricity, centripetality, and centrifugality and causes distributions of activities around the fire according to an ordinary scale. Examples handed down by people worldwide show that producing, taming and using of fire means to have great power and to control acts of production, transformation and destruction (Chevalier and Gheerbrant, 1996: 483; Lewis-Williams, 2005: 101, 181-189; Salokoski, 2006: 194; Wilson, 1988: 27, 42). The fire-place and the hearth according to the traditions of ancient cultures and archaeological records symbolizes the act of creation, which inherent contains birth and death, and is related to the origin of both individuals and the community, but also the whole world (Freidel, Schele, and Parker 1993: 130, 178; Reichel-Dolmatoff, 1978: 80-81). Often the hearth is regarded as a symbol of the sexual intercourse and union of man and woman or the male and the female powers, which set up and move the whole world. People thought that making fire by drilling a stick into a wooden plate imitates the creative coition and the origin of both, the world and man. That explained the importance of fire-rituals across different cultures (King, 2002: 157; Salokoski, 2006: 193-194). The fire-drilling procedure however was recognized also looking at the rotation of the sun and the whole sky around the polar axis, modelled by the shadow-stick as a phallus upon the plane of the ground, which resembles a vulva (Parpola, 1985: 117; Rappenglück, 2005b: 160-161). According to the ancient conceptions the drilling world-axis and the rotating sun, both symbols of the heaven, exerted their power upon the susceptible earth, producing and preserving the life in the world. Thus it is understandable why people thought that the fire-place represents a creative womb, which they compared and related to the sun as symbol for the celestial source of power in the world (Parpola, 1985: 88, 159; Rabuzzi, 1987: 4106; Turnbull, 1985: 45). The close relation of the female principal to the fire-place/hearth is reflected in the performance of special fire-rituals carried out by woman within the domestic space (Elsona and Smith, 2001; Zeidler 1984: 435-443). A derivative of such ideas is the identification of the fire-place or hearth with both, the navel of the human body and the centre of the world, which denote the origin of transformational physical and spiritual power Chevalier and Gheerbrant, 1996: 718-719; Müller, 1982: 101; Schroeter, 1998: 28, 34, 35). Thus according to the ancient people the place at which a fire is kindled offers the possibility to get in contact with the primordial origin of the cosmos and to communicate with the ancestors, which are present there (Gulløv and Appelt, 2001: 158). That leads to a further interpretation of the custom to put certain objects, such as bones, clay balls, animal or human figurines, intentional near or into the fire. The deposits may have served in acts of cooking, heating of water, making ceramic, and others. Traditions of cultures however show that people used the deposit of objects in around and in the fire-place to relate themselves to the chain of ancestors, which is bound to the origin of the cosmos and to get in contact with the spirits. The Kwara'ae in Africa, the Maya in Mesoamerica, the Dakota in North America, the Dravidian and the Indus-Culture in India or the Tibetan for example put "sacred stones", mostly three or four, into a hearth (McKhann, 1992: 164; Müller, 1970: 212, 1956: 177; Parpola, 1985: 56, 84, 88, 159; Stein, 2001: 159; Welchman-Gegeo and Watson-Gegeo, 2001: 68-69). A similar ritual act might have existed in Çatalhöyük (Hodder, 2006; 120-121). Thus the fire-place and hearth anchored a family or a clan at a place, giving life, protection, stability, unity, and ensuring the linkage and communication with the ancestral domain or even the powerful centre of the world itself. The position of fire-altars in the dwellings, close to the centre and the main supporter, if one exists, follows a similar symbolism (Parpola, 1985: 116). In addition ancient people regarded the smoke raising up from the fire-place/altar as a symbol of verticality, joining together and relating to each other the cosmic strata between heaven and earth (Chevalier and Gheerbrant, 1996: 889-890). The column of smoke, embodying spiritual power, was considered as another kind of visualizing the world-axis. The smoke outlet in a tent or a house opened the membrane of the roof to align the dwelling to the highest point in the sky and at the same time to make the structure in principle susceptible for celestial powers, such as light, wind or rain. Ancient traditions proof the importance of the outlet, which is called a "window, door or well of the sky" (Stein, 2001: 143-157). In certain cases the outlet is not only the exit for the smoke, but the single entrance to the structure (Stein, 2001: 157-167), as in the case of Çatalhöyük buildings (Lewis-Williams, 2005: 107-108). Though this actual is troublesome for accessing the dwelling, it parallelizes the path into the man-made structure with the axis mundi of the smoke column.

CENTRICITY AND THE AXIS MUNDI

Ancient people thought that the centre, in which the world-axis is set, is a storage of creation and pure dynamic intensity, a point at which opposing forces and domains, such as life and death, female and male, the material and the spiritual world, are meeting and intersecting each other, coexisting and balanced in harmony (Rappenglück, 2005b). Cosmogonical myths often illustrate how, starting from the point of the origin, the cosmic realms, directions, and strata are unfolded and arranged around it. Only at the centre of the world it is possible to get in contact with creative power and knowledge. The setting-out of creation from the centre into the space implies a zenithal world-axis, which is given by the human sense for gravity and fixed as the vertical line between zenith, location and nadir. This fundamentally defines a tripartite cosmos, consisting of the earth in the centre, and the polarity of the lower and the upper world. That way the idea of a spectrum of increasing or decreasing cosmic power, flowing up and down along the world-axis and the movements and interactions between a spiritual and a material realm was illustrated. The world-axis holds up and connects, but also pierces the hierarchically layered cosmic domains, which were considered to be "other worlds", and often equated with different physical and psychical levels. Representations of the certain landscapes and the plants, animals, humans or gods living there signify the respective strata (Müller, 1982: 74; Rappenglück, 2005b: 157-161; Reichel, 1998: 35-47, 63; Reichel-Dolmatoff, 1978: 80; Traube, 1986: 67). Thus the world-axis was regarded as a way to reach and to travel through the hierarchical layered, but coexisting realms of the universe. Sensitive persons, for example shamans, and rulers tried to reside at the middle of the world, to access cosmic power and knowledge for their purposes. Ordinary people also hoped to participate in the forces of the centre and therefore settled closely nearby. At locations, which were recognized as the centre, sensitive persons (for example shamans) fell in ecstasy, rulers were enthroned, jurisdiction took place, sacrifices were carried out, and meeting places, houses, shrines, temples or cities were founded (Rappenglück, 2005b; Werness, 2000: 69, 168-169, 173, 227). Frequently structures have been set upon one single post to symbolize the world turning around the polar world-axis (Naumann, 1971: 108, 190, 246-247, 250). The main, strong supporter of a structure, in particular of a dwelling, was regularly considered as an axis mundi (Fox, 1993: 15; Naumann, 1971: 53-66, 96, 189, 196; Reichel-Dolmatoff, 1978: 80-81). Often such a post or pillar completely or partially shows a quadrangular shape, which symbolizes not only vertical, but also horizontal axiality. It indicates the cardinal directions to the important spatiotemporal domains, containing certain powers, objects, qualities, and ancestors in the world, and align the parts of the enclosed human habitat to them (McKhann, 1992: 157; Müller, 1982: 95; Werness, 2000: 177). A similar symbolism can be assigned to certain objects, such as remains of plants, animals, humans, food, masks, and other things, which charged with mythological meaning are located at special places close to the main supporter or fixed upon his surface, if they follow the principle of cardinality. Additional supporters, occasionally equipped with special masks or depictions, put at the corners of a structure hold up the world at the cardinal points. Frequently they are associated with the main powers, world-quarters, colors, plants, animals, gods, the ancestors (Müller, 1982: 74-77; Naumann, 1971; Schroeter, 1998: 76-77, 100-101; Wer-ness, 2000: 199-200, 227). These carry the world and act as guardians, are related to seasonality, ensure the cycle of life and death, and protect the descendants in the living community. The supporter can be imagined also as tree, a mountain, and as ladder, to symbolize the cosmic strata around the world-axis (McKhann, 1992: 168, 171; Müller, 1982: 102; Naumann, 1971: 189, 194; Werness, 2000: 5-56, 134, 168-169, 177, 227, 232, 296).

ORGANIZING THE WORLD AS A HOME

The partitions of the vertical and horizontal strata followed social, psychical, religious, and natural properties (Griaule, 1966: 101-110; Müller, 1970: 130-222; Reichel-Dolmatoff, 1978; Schroeter, 1998: 25; Traube, 1986: 67). The latter were founded in the ecosystem (Reichel-Dolmatoff, 1978), topographical (Lehner, 2006: 130-138), and astronomical conditions (Rappenglück, 1999, 2005b). Rivers for example often served as demarcation between the ancestral world and the world of the living (Gulløv and Appelt, 2001: 158; McKhann, 1992: 163) or guided the location of structures downstream/upstream (Werness, 2000: 332). The spatiotemporal courses of sun, moon, and the stars especially helped to trigger the perception of directionality and rhythm of life in cultures worldwide (Krupp, 1983; Lehner, 2006: 57-64, 107-130; Rabuzzi, 1987: 4105; Rappenglück, 1999, 2005b; Reichel, 1998: 60-67; Reichel-Dolmatoff, 1978; Ruggles, 1999; Woodward and Lewis, 1998: 308-310, 316).

For organizing the world as a home it was essential to set and respect physic, psychic and social enclosures. These allowed to structure and direct activities, to concentrate physical and mental power, to establish and to protect a steady state of human life (Werness, 2001: 135). The concept of a semipermeable membrane (Lewis-Williams, 2002, 2005: 110-113; Rappenglück, 2005a) represented by rock faces in the caves, walls in artificial buildings, and non-domestic structures, such as stone circles, offered humans spatiotemporal enclosures (Krupp, 1983: 217). Setting an enclosure founded a first partition, which separates an outer from an inner living space (exosphere/endosphere; Müller, K.E., 1987)), the wild and the domestic sphere, proximity and distance, kinship and foreign parts, the sacred and the profane, and other dichotomies (Barnatt, 1998; McKhann, 1992: 160, 164; Müller, E., 1987). The openings in the membrane and the partition within the enclosure, a dwelling for example, follows sets of binaries. They divide the spatiotemporal landscape, and the whole range of objects, living beings, events, properties, social relationships, myths and rituals, spiritual powers of the world into paired opposites (Egenter, 2004; Müller, 1956; Naumann, 1971: 199-203; Rabuzzi, 1987: 4104; Reichel-Dolmatoff, 1987; Schroeter, 1998: 76-77; Werness, 2000: 25, 291-292).

Places of transition are given by openings in the membrane, such as the doors and the windows in a structure (McKhann, 1992: 161; Werness, 2000: 87, 227). There the spatiotemporal organisation of the building gets transparent and other strata of the world are accessible, but being placed on the threshold is dangerous and unsure.

Rituals of founding, renewal, and dedication served to vivify the structure, in particular a dwelling, by cosmic powers, to establish order and to animate the living space (Stuart, 1998: 395). The building is considered to be a living being, which in some cases is designed as a giant animal, a man or a woman (Eisler, 1910: 723, fn. 8; Griaule, 1966: 101-110; Müller, 1982: 167-168, 170-174; Rabuzzi, 1987: 4104; Stuart, 1998: 395; Werness, 2000: 87, 134, 199, 238, 296). Its construction elements correspond to the body parts of the cosmic creature. In particular ancient people thought that its framework is closely related to the ancestors, which found, guided, protected the clan through time and space (Griaule, 1966: 40-56, 101-107, 109-124; Rabuzzi, 1987: 4106; Werness, 2000: 68-69). Thus the building as a whole or in its parts must be tamed, treated with care, periodically purified and fed (Stuart, 1998: 393; Werness, 2001: 135). Ritual processions related to the structures and the landscape, time-factored by the biotope or astronomical phenomena, served to animate and empower the house and to renew cosmogony (Barnatt, 1998: 93, 96; Müller, 1982: 79-80, 125, 166).

Thus ancient people worldwide considered caves Rappenglück, 1999, 2005a), non-domestic architecture (Egenter, 1980, 1989; Krupp, 1997; Ruggles, 1999), dwellings, such as a tent, a hut, a house, a temple or a tomb (Eisler, 1910: 600-632; Frank, 2001: 140-1443; Griaule, 1966: 40-56, 101-107, 109-124; Hentze, 1961; Hultkrantz, 1987: 285-290; Krupp, 1983, 1997; McKhann, 1992; Müller, 1956: 280-283, 296-318, 1982: 74; Naumann, 1971: 78-101, 174-182, 204-209; Rabuzzi, 1987: 4105; Schroeter, 1998-73; Stein, 2001: 120-253; Taube, 1998: 427-478; Traube, 1986: 66; Werness, 2000: 164-165, 183, 197), but in an extension also a village or a city (Griaule, 1966: 107-109; Müller, 1956: 139, 143-187, 261; Whitley, 1971) and finally the landscape (Barnatt, 1998: 92-105; Krupp, 1997; Lewis and Stout, 1998; Ruggles, 1999; Wesson, 93-122; Woodward and Lewis, 1998: 24-48, 229-237, 301-326, 330-340, 353-416, 423-442) as replica of the cosmos, which reflect concepts of cosmology and cosmogony in the human habitat.

LEPENKSI VIR

A good example for cosmographic symbolism showing some of the features presented above can be found at Lepenski Vir, 7000-6000 cal BC. (Rappenglück, 1995): There the dwellings had been constructed as trapezoids, according to geometrical rules and astronomical aligning along the cardinal points. At the centre of each building, a special stone close to the hearth, was intentionally set. The structures were grouped following a binary division upstream and downstream (Radovanović, 2000: 339). The dead had been buried so that their body with flexed legs formed a trapezoid, which parallelized the shape of the houses and also was aligned to the cardinal points. From the way of construction one can derive a "ritual of the rope", which is known from the old Indian scripture of the Śulbasūtras, 5th c. BC. and related to cosmomagical rituals.

CONCLUSION: COSMOGRAPHIC SYMBOLISM AND THE HUMAN MIND

Cosmographic symbolism seems to be a relevant idea for the interpretation of some archaeological remains of the Neolithic (Lewis-Williams, 2005) and also for the Palaeolithic (Rappenglück, 1999; 2005a). The basics for that symbolism seem to be preformed at a subhuman level: Pongids, Bonobos, are able to use a system of signs to indicate the direction of the path they have taken to other members of their group. It has also been demonstrated that Gorillas, construct their night camps observing a special spatial order, which allowed them to control the environment (Egenter, 2001: 53-55). The knowledge of spatial values, such as centre, periphery, proximity and distance, verticality, and accessibility is obvious. But since the time the species homo learned the handling of fire, there appears a very new intercourse with the ecosphere: Based on the special functionality of his self-consciousness and parallel to the progressive reduction of instincts man was aware of a certain kind of separation from the ordinary world. The anthropological concept of "eccentricity" (Plessner, 1975: 288-346) very well describes his feeling to be not really centred and somehow out of natural order. To establish and to keep himself and his culture steady state and to integrate and orientate himself and his habitat anew into the ecosystem, man tried to change wilderness (chaos) into culture (cosmos) and to substitute the unknown by the well-known (Bollnow, 1980: 61-62; Müller, E., 1987: 3-66;

Peterson, 1999; Rabuzzi, 1987: 4107). Thus he turned his eccentricity into centricity (Bollnow, 1980: 58-61, 123-125). Because man seem to essentially need re-centring, he developed certain cognitive models, which as a core element contained the semantic of cosmographic symbolism. They also served to answer his fundamental questions concerning the structure of the world and the riddles of life and death. That way man considered ecospheres as a well-ordered, domesticated and habitable domains, as a home to dwell.

References

BOIVIN, N. (2004) - Landscape and Cosmology in the South Indian Neolithic: New Perspectives on the Deccan Ashmounds. *Cambridge Archaeological Journal*. Cambridge. 14:2, p. 235-257.

BOLLNOW, O. F. (^{4}1980) - *Mensch und Raum*. Stuttgart: Kohlhammer. 310 p.

BRADLEY, R. (2002) - *The Past in prehistoric societies*. London: Routlege. 192 p.

CHEVALIER, J.; GHEERBRANT, A. (1996) – *Dictionary of Symbols*. London: Penguin, p. 1178.

EGENTER, N. (1980) - Bauform als Zeichen und Symbol. Nichtdomestikales Bauen im japanischen Volkskult. Zürich: ETH.

EGENTER, N. (1989) - The Master of the Wilderness, the bear, lives in the upper part of our home. House and World-view of the Ainu. Zürich: Documentation Office for Fundamental Studies in Building Theory. 25 p.

EGENTER, N. (2001) - The Deep Structure of Architecture: Constructivity and Human evolution. In AMERLINCK, M.-J., ed. - *Architectural Anthropology. Outlines of a constructive anthropology*. Westport, Connecticut/London: Bergin & Garvey. Architectural Anthropology 6, p. 43-81.

EISLER, R. (1910) - Weltenmantel und Himmelszelt. Religionswissenschaftliche Untersuchungen zur Urgeschichte des antiken Weltbildes. 2 Bde. München: C. H. Beck'sche Verlagsbuchhandlung Oskar Beck.

ELSONA, C. M.; SMITH, M. E. (2001) - Archaeological deposits from the Aztec New Fire ceremony. *Ancient Mesoamerica*. New York N.Y.: 12, p.157–174.

FOX, J. J. (1993) - Comparative Perspectives on Austronesian Houses: An introductory essay. In FOX, J. J. ed. - *Inside Austronesian Houses, Perspectives on Domestic Designs for Living*. Canberra: Australian National University, p. X -28.

FRANK, R. M. (2001) - Hunting the European sky-bears: the Candlemas Bear Day and World Renewal ceremonies. Astronomy, Cosmology, and Landscape. In RUGGLES, C.; PRENDERGAST, F.; RAY, T., eds. Borgnor Regis: Ocarina Books, p. 133-157 (Proceedings of the SEAC 98 Meeting, Dublin, Ireland, September 1998).

FREIDEL, D.; SCHELE, L.; PARKER, J. (1993) - *Maya Cosmos: Three Thousand Years on the Shaman's Path*. New York: Morrow. 543 p.

GLENN, M. (2003) - Architecture demonstrates power. BA thesis, Haverford College.

GRIAULE, M. (1966) - *Dieu d' Eau*. Paris: Arthème Fayard. 220 p.

GULLØV, H. C.; APPELT, M. (2001) - Social bonding and shamanism among Late Dorset groups in High Arctic Greenland. In PRICE, N., ed. - *The Archaeology of Shamanism*. London and New York: Routledge, p. 147-162.

HENTZE, C. (1961) - *Das Haus als Weltort der Seele*. Stuttgart: Ernst Klett. 179 p.

HODDER, I. (2006) - *The Leopard's Tale. Revealing the Mysteries of Çatalhöyük*. London: Thames & Hudson. 288 p.

HULTKRANTZ, A. (1987) - Diversity in Cosmology: The Case of the Wind River Shoshoni. *The Canadian Journal of Native Studies*. Brandon. VII, 2, p. 279-295.

KRUPP, E. C. (1983) - *Echoes of the Ancient Skies. The Astronomy of Lost Civilizations*. New York, Oxford: Oxford University Press. 386 p.

KRUPP, E. C. (1997) - *Skywatchers, Shamans & Kings. Astronomy and the Archaeology of Power*. New York: John Wiley. 364 p.

LEHNER, E. (2006) - *Ideen und Konzepte der Architektur in außereuropäischen Kulturen*. Wien, Graz: Neuer Wissenschaftlicher Verlag. 223 p.

LEWIS-WILLIAMS, D. (2002) - *The Mind in the Cave: Consciousness and the Origins of Art*. London: Thames & Hudson, 320 p.

LEWIS-WILLIAMS, D. (2004) - Constructing a cosmos: architecture, power and domestification at Çatalhöyük. *Journal of Social Archaeology*. Thousand Oaks, CA. 4, p. 28-59.

LEWIS-WILLIAMS, D.; PEARCE, D. (2005) - *Inside the Neolithic Mind. Consciousness, Cosmos and the Realm of the Gods*. London: Thames & Hudson, 320 p.

McKHANN, C. F. (1992) - Fleshing out the Bones: The Cosmic and Social Dimensions of Space in Naxi Architecture, Ph.D. Thesis in Anthropology, University of Chicago.

MÜLLER, K. E. (1987) - *Das Magische Universum der Identität. Elementarformen soziologischen Verhaltens, ein ethnologischer Grundriss*. Frankfurt, New York. 475 p.

MÜLLER, W. (1956) - *Die Religionen der Waldlandindianer Nordamerikas*. Berlin: Dietrich Reimer. 392 p.

MÜLLER, W. (1970) - *Glauben und Denken der Sioux. Zur Gestalt archaischer Weltbilder*. Berlin: Dietrich Reimer. 419 p.

NAS, P.J. M.; BRAKUS, C. (2004) - The dancing house instances of the human body in city and architecture. In SOHEILA SHAHSHAHANI ed. - *Body as medium of meaning*. Muenster, Lit Verlag, p. 27-56.

NAUMANN, N. (1971) - Das Umwandeln des Himmelspfeilers: ein japanischer Mythos und seine kulturhistorische Einordnung. *Asian Folklore Studies*. Tokyo 5, 292 p.

PARPOLA, A. (1985) - The Sky-Garment. A study of the Harrapan religion and its relation to the Mesopotamian and later Indian religions. *Studia Orientalia*. Helsinki. 57, 216 p.

PEARSON, M. P.; RICHARDS, C. (1994) - Ordering the World: Perceptions of Architecture, Space, and Time. In PARKER, M.; RICHARDS, C., eds. - *Architecture and Order: Approaches to Social Space*. London: Routledge, p. 1–37.

PLESSNER, H. (^{3}1975) - *Die Stufen des Organischen und der Mensch. Einleitung in die Philosophische Anthropologie*. Berlin, New York: De Gruyter, 373 p.

PETERSON, J. B. (1999) - *Maps of Meaning: The Architecture of Belief*. New York and London: Routledge. 541 p.

RABUZZI, K. A. (1987) - Home. In Encyclopedia of Religion, second edition, p. 4104-4107.

RAPPENGLÜCK, M. A. (1995) - Lepenksi Vir vor 7000 Jahren: Messen mit Schnur und Stab. *In Zur Geschichte des Vermessungswesens*. Wiesbaden: Chmielorz. (VDV-Schriftenreihe, Der Vermessungsingenieur in der Praxis; 8), p. 8-10.

RAPPENGLÜCK, M. A. (2005a) - The Cave as a Cosmos: Cave Art, Cosmography and Shamanism in the Upper Palaeolithic. In VETROV, V., ED. - *Iskusstvo i ritual lednikovoi epochi*. Lugansk: YP Vega, p. 126-144.

RAPPENGLÜCK, M. A. (2005b) - The Pivot of the Cosmos: The Concepts of the World Axis across Cultures. In KÕIVA, M.; PUSTYLNIK, I.; VESIK, L., eds. - *Cosmic Catastrophes. A collection of Articles*. Tartu: European Society for Astronomy in Cultures, p. 157-165.

RUGGLES, C. (1999) - *Astronomy in Prehistoric Britain and Ireland*. New Haven and London: Yale University Press, 285 p.

REICHEL, E. (1998) - Die Öko-Politik im Schamanismus der Yukuna und Tanimuka vom nordwestlichen Amazonas. In GOTTWALD, F.-T.; RÄTSCH, C., eds. - *Schamanische Wissenschaften: Ökologie, Naturwissenschaft und Kunst*. München: Diederichs, p. 25-95.

REICHEL-DOLMATOFF, G. (1978) - The Loom of Life: A Kogi Principle of Integration. *Journal of Latin American Lore*. Los Angeles, CA. 4 (1), p. 5-27.

SALOKOSKI, M. (2006) - How Kings are made – How kingship changes. A study of rituals and ritual change in pre-colonial and colonial Owamboland,Namibia research series in anthropology University of Helsinki, Dissertation, p. 335.

SCHROETER, W. (1998) - Indianische Wohnformen. Vom Tipi zum Pueblo. Vom Wickiup zum Hogan. Vom Langhaus zur Earth Lodge. Wyk auf Föhr: Verlag für Amerikanistik. 132 p.

STEIN, R. A. (1987) - *Le monde en petit: jardins en miniature et habitations dans la pensée religieuse d'Extrême-Orient*. Paris: Flammarion. 345 p.

STUART, D. (1998) - *"The Fire Enters His House": Architecture and Ritual in Classic Maya Texts*. Washington, D.C.: Dumbarton Oaks Research Library and Collection. 562 p.

TAUBE, K. (1998) - The Jade Hearth: Centrality, Rulership, and the Classic Maya Temple. In HOUSTON, S.D., ed. - *Function and Meaning in Classic Maya Architecture*. Washington D.C.: Dumbarton Oaks Research Library and Collection, p. 427-478.

TRAUBE, E. G. (1986) - *Cosmology and Social Life. Ritual Exchange among the Mambai of East Timor*. Chicago, London: The University of Chicago Press. 289 p.

WELCHMAN GEGEO, D.; WATSON-GEGEO, K.A. (2001) - Villagers Doing Indigenous Epistemology. *The Contemporary Pacific*. Honolulu, 13/1, p. 55–88.

WERNESS, H. B. (2000) -*The Continuum Encyclopedia of Native Art. Worldview, Symbolism & Culture in Africa, Oceania & Native North America*. New York, London: Continuum. 360 p.

WHEATLEY, P. (1971) - *The Pivot of the four quarters, A preliminary enquiry into the origins and character of the ancient Chinese City*. Edinburgh: Edinburgh University Press. 602 p.

WHITRIDGE, P. (2004) - Landscapes, Houses, Bodies, Things: "Place" and the Archaeology of Inuit Imaginaries. *Journal of Archaeological Method and Theory* . New York 11/2, p. 213-250.

WILSON, P. J. (1988) - *The Domestication of the Human Species*. New Haven: Yale University Press.

WOODWARD, D.; LEWIS. G. M., eds. (1998) - The History of Cartography, Vol. 2. Chicago and London: University of Chicago Press.

ZEIDLER, J. (1984) - Social Space in Valdivia Society: Community Patterning and Domestic Structure at Real Alto, *3000–2000 B.C.* Ph.D. dissertation, University of Illinois.

THE SHIP AND ITS SYMBOLISM IN THE EUROPEAN BRONZE AGE

Andrea VIANELLO

University of Oxford, a_vianello@hotmail.com

Abstract: For thousands of years, boats and ships have been depicted on objects and structures and continue to be powerful and instantly recognisable images in the contemporary world. While several European Bronze Age cultures adopted the image of the ship as a recurring leitmotiv, different meanings became to be associated with these images. It is often possible to recognise the arrival of foreign ideas and their inclusion in existing cultures. A possible common origin for the European artistic repertoire will be investigated.
Keywords: *ship; boat; symbolism; Europe; Bronze Age.*

Résumé: Pour des milliers d'années, les bateaux ont été dépeints sur des objets et des structures et continuent à être des images puissantes et immédiatement reconnaissables dans le monde contemporain. Pendant que plusieurs cultures de l'âge du bronze européenne adoptaient l'image du bateau comme leitmotiv se reproduisant, différentes significations ont été associées à ces images. C'est souvent possible de reconnaître l'arrivée d'idées étrangères et leur inclusion dans les cultures existantes. Une origine commune possible pour le répertoire artistique européen sera étudiée.
Mots clés: *navire, bateau, symbolisme, Europe, âge du Bronze.*

INTRODUCTION

The image of the ship recurs in all inhabited regions from ancient times. There is scientific evidence that boats were used at least 40.000 years ago, and possibly much earlier (McGrail, 2003: 3–4). Having been such a feature in the lives of men and women for so long, boats and ships have become an integral part of human activity, and it is hardly surprising that they have been depicted over the course of history.

The interpretation of the material evidence relating to the depictions of ships has followed separate lines of enquiry, mainly following a distinction based on the medium, and, to a lesser extent, geographical distribution. For instance, studies of Scandinavian rock art have largely ignored depictions on bronzes or boat-shaped graves. The geographical distribution of the types of archaeological evidence overlaps only to a minimal extent (Kaul, 1998: 113). However, all Scandinavian representations are stylistically connected; this is demonstrated by the chronology of rock art imagery based on the scientific dating of bronzes on which similar depictions have been found (Kaul, 1998: 87–90). Bradley (2006) argues that the cosmology recognised by Kaul (1998) as underpinning the representations on bronzes may also be recognised on rock art depictions, and he proposes further research to test the compatibility of the cosmology with rock art images.

Another school of thought (Kristiansen, 2004; Kristiansen and Larsson, 2005: 189–212) recognises ships as symbols, and as such they are compared with similar symbols across the European continent and the Mediterranean, ignoring any boundaries.

Interpreting the material evidence attached to the iconography of the ship requires a balance between contextual analyses of images as part of broader landscapes, but it is also necessary to consider foreign cultural influences. The latter cannot properly be understood if the meanings of the images within their contexts are unknown. The comparison between similar symbols in different cultures cannot be limited to stylistic analyses of the graphical representations. Bredholt Christensen and Warburton (2004) argue that, in archaeology, 'a symbol must be an expression of something (Saussure) and it must be recognizable (Peirce)' by at least two people. Frequent meanings should be inferable from the archaeological evidence: similarity in contexts and consumption patterns may be a valid indication of similarity among a given set of symbols, even before any deciphering of meaning[1] is attempted, bearing in mind that it is not necessarily possible to decode what a symbol meant in antiquity (Bredholt Christensen and Warburton, 2004).

GOBUSTAN AND THE BIRTH OF A REPERTOIRE

The earliest depictions of ships in the European and Mediterranean regions can be found near Gobustan, Azerbaijan (Figure 4.1b). The chronology of these rock carvings is still debated, ranging, for the depictions of boats, between the 6th millennium BC and the 16th millennium (Farajova, pers. comm.). Representations of boats appear amongst a multitude of wild animals and human figures; no relationship between scenes can be recognised. Interestingly, the sun occasionally appears associated with the boats and a solar myth has been proposed by Formozov (1980: 38-39). Around Gobustan rock art is spread over a wide area, but significantly boats appear only on panels found in the two areas closest to the

---
[1] McCauley and Lawson (2002, 9–10) suggest that knowledge of meaning may not be indispensable in a ritual, even for the participants.

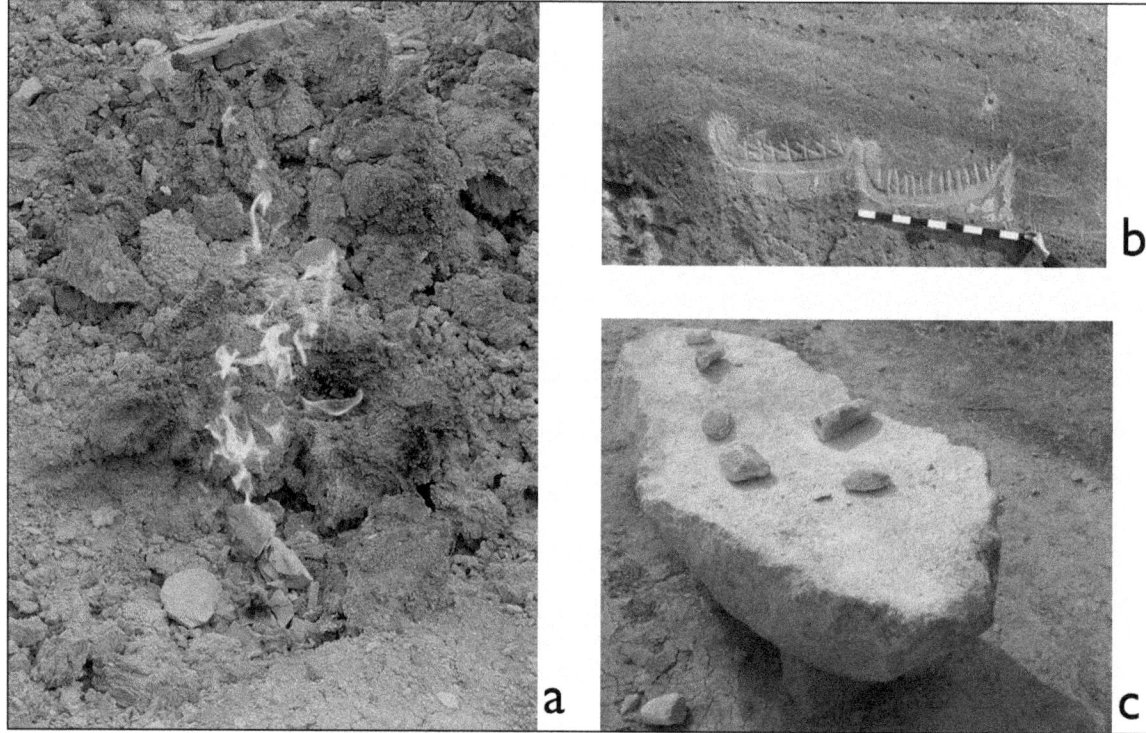

Fig. 4.1. Gobustan, (a) self-igniting fire at Lokbatan mud volcano, © Bundesanstalt für Geowissenschaften und Rohstoffe (BGR); (b) carved ships, © Malahat Farajova; (c) stone tambourine.

Caspian Sea, on the Boyukdash and Kichikdash mountains (Farajova, 2004). Some of the boats depicted can be large: one is 150 cm long (Anati, 2001). However, many other rock carvings are also large – such as a fish (cetacean) about five metres long. Large depictions appear characteristic of the most ancient periods and may date to the Palaeolithic. This would suggest that Gobustan might be the region where old beliefs involving boats formed, possibly over a period spanning from the Mesolithic to the Bronze Age (if the large boat rock carvings are earlier). The location, a region of mud volcanoes, appears to have been used for ritual purposes probably because features of sky, sea, land, and fire could all be seen together. The presence of both sea fish and boats among the rock carvings, and their location close to the ancient shoreline, demonstrate that these depictions were probably representations of real boats. The Caspian Sea was connected to the Black Sea through a narrow passage, and from there, at the time of the first rock carvings, it was possible to reach the Mediterranean. Therefore the area must then have been more important for maritime traffic than in later periods.

The ancient landscape of Gobustan must have been truly extraordinary: there were mountains reaching into the sky towards the sun; volcanoes spewing fire (Figure 4.1a), mud, smoke and steam; cold rain, and rivers running. In such a scenario, populated by a variety of figures, all the human senses would have been stimulated[2] and it would,

perhaps, have been possible to actually see boats reaching towards the horizon, without any need of the imagination; in other words, these were not 'symbolic' ships.

The artistic repertoire developed over thousands of years in the Gobustan region, and at least some of the associated beliefs must have spread into the European continent. Gobustan was on an important ancient route connecting the Near East to Asia.

EGYPT

In Egypt, model ships often featured in the funerary assemblages of elite burials ever since Old Kingdom times (Grajetzki, 2003: 40–41). By the First Dynasty, actual ships appeared in the boat-grave cemetery at Abydos, dated to 3300–3100 BC (Ward, 2006). In the second half of the fourth millennium, boats become a frequent subject on painted Naqada II pottery (Wilkinson, 1999), rock carvings at Wadi Abbad (Ward, 2006: 120), and in Tomb 100 at Nekhen (Hierakonpolis; Cialowicz,

---

[2] There are at least two stones in the area, the so-called 'stone tambourines' (Figure 1c). They produce metallic notes, of variable musical tones, when struck. The stones demonstrate that sensory stimulations were a key component of ancient rituals in the area. McCauley and Lawson (2002, 77–79) suggest that prolonged emotional stimulation may produce subconscious effects that help enhance perception of the experience and memorize it. Rock art, perhaps, would have been used here as a means to help memorize events. In some cases, an excess of emotional stimulation could affect mnemonic capabilities and produce a state of altered consciousness (McCauley and Lawson 2002, 80–81), but such a state is not evident in the naturalistic depictions of boats.

Fig. 4.2. pyramid of Unas, (a) antechamber, west (left) and north (right) wall and ceiling decorated with stars; (b) boat pits; (c) relief in the causeway, after Verner.

1995), but these artistic manifestations are associated with the arrival of people from Lower Egypt by boat.

Ships have been interpreted as symbols of royal power (Williams; 1988: 38). The first occurrence of ships in a symbolic context is to be found in the Pyramid Texts – inscribed in the pyramid of Unas (Kaul, 2005), the last Fifth-Dynasty pharaoh. Utterance 267 reads, 'he flies as a goose; he alights as a scarab upon the empty throne which is in thy boat, O Rē' (…) [Unas] pushes off from the earth in thy boat, O Rē'; so when thou goest forth from the horizon, he [Unas] has his sceptre in his hand, as navigator of thy boat, O Rē''(Mercer, 1952: 89). The idea that the pharaoh would ascend to the sun in the sky is repeated throughout the texts, but his means of so doing vary from text to text, and not all the 'spells' were part of Egyptian mainstream belief. Further elements of this belief can be gathered from Unas' pyramid (Figure 4.2a), which is part of a larger mortuary temple, where two structures in the form of boats (Figure 4.2b), and possibly also containing wooden boats, could either have symbolized the diurnal and nocturnal vessels of the sun god (Verner, 2002: 337–338), or the boats that carried the construction materials for the monument and which were depicted in the causeway[3] (Figure 4.2c). The texts were inscribed to be read from the burial chamber to the antechamber, understood as the 'horizon', and would have accompanied the deceased pharaoh from the tomb to the sun, a journey also symbolized by the architecture (Verner, 2002: 43).

Verner (2002, 41) warns that Pyramid Texts 'compile various conceptions of the beyond, drawn from different origins and periods'. In utterances 273 and 274, there is a reference to cannibalism, '[Unas] is he who eats men and lives on gods, lords of messengers, who distributes orders' (Mercer, 1952: 93), a practice which was not followed in Egypt. The Pyramid Texts were a collection of accounts circulating at the time, assembled to ensure that the pharaoh was sure of reaching his final destination, the sun, one way or another. The possibility that the symbolic boats of the Pyramid Texts might have been a foreign influence is suggested by the fact that there is no reference to water: the journey of the boat is set in the sky, and stars are depicted in the burial chamber, antechamber (Figure 4.2a), and corridor[4] (Verner, 2002: 334). However, a boat travelling to the horizon, where it meets the sun, is actually used, and this appears in contradiction to the astronomical references on the ceiling of the same burial chamber and antechamber where the Pyramid Texts are written. That view recalls the landscape of Gobustan, where it seems that the horizon met all earthly things, and boats were present in that landscape. The Egyptians may have favoured the use of a boat as the most suitable means of transportation for a pharaoh, and therefore adapted to their needs the circulating belief that

---

[3] The accompanying inscription reads, '[I brought granite pillars from?] Elephantine for his majesty Unas within seven days (…) His majesty praised me for this.'

[4] The stars in the burial chamber and the antechamber point to the zenith; those in the corridor point to the north, evidencing a complex astronomical alignment of the monument with the sky.

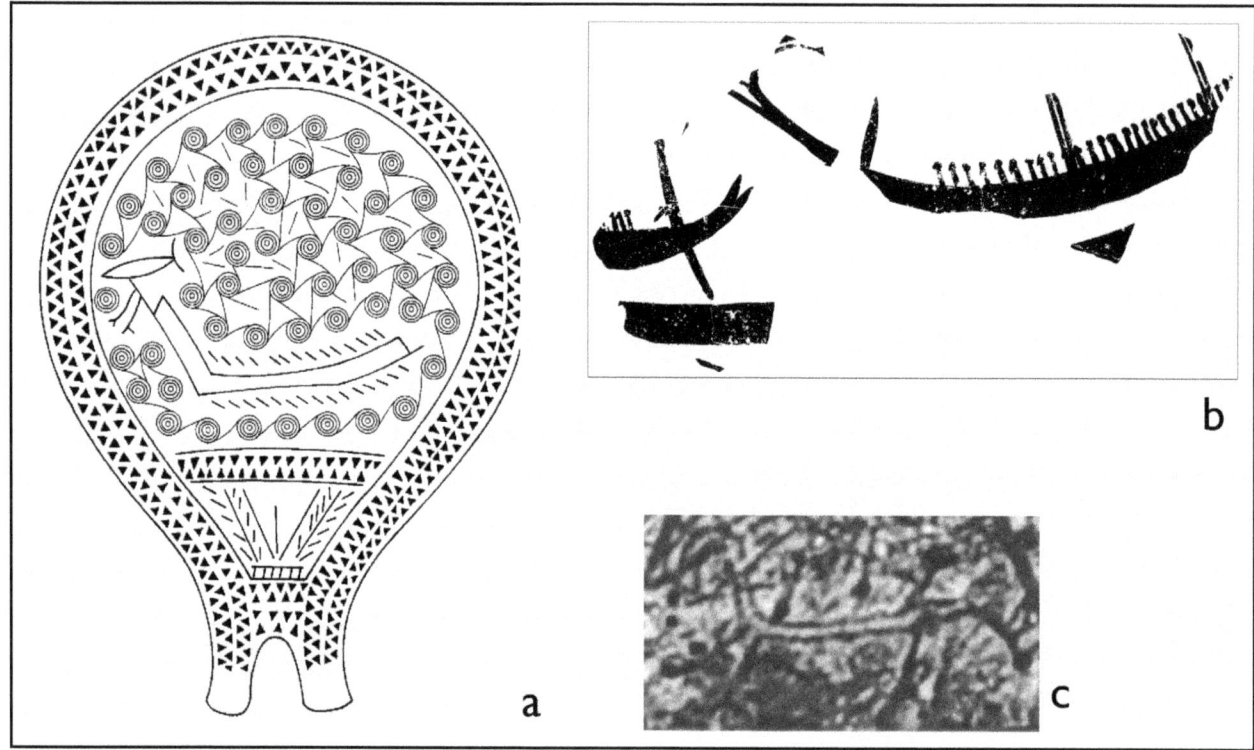

Fig. 4.3. Aegean depictions of boats, (a) 'frying pan' from tomb 174, Chalandriani; (b) boat from Middle Helladic potsherds from Aegina, after Siedentopf; (c) carved ship at Folia, © HERAC, photograph by G. Dimitriadis.

overemphasized the role of the ship as the only means of transportation capable of such a journey.

THE MEDITERRANEAN

Boats in the Mediterranean also appear in later periods. Rock art boats at Folia (Figure 4.3c), Greece (Dimitriadis, pers. comm.), may date to the Early Helladic period; boats with fishes were depicted on Early Cycladic II 'frying pans'. These boats may have represented the process of fishing, and, by association, also life and death; the repertoire of the sun and boat is also featured and may have represented the cycle of day and night. These possible meanings and the shape of the vessels point to the cycle of fertility. The 'wheel cross' also appears on these vessels (Davis, 1992: 717, figure 9), and from the site of Chalandriani[5] (Figure 4.3a) there are examples depicting oared ships, with fish emblems on their high prows (Hekman, 2003).

As the Mycenaean exchange network spreads across the Mediterranean (Vianello, 2005), a few representations appear on Mycenaean pottery, especially the Middle Helladic examples found at Kolonna on Aegina (Siedentopf, 1991); these representations echo the depictions found on the Cycladic 'frying pans' (Rutter, 1993: 779). Ships with bird protomes (Figure 4.3b) have been found in the same Aeginetan contexts since the Middle Helladic (Hiller, 1972; Wachsmann, 2000). The only possible depiction on Urnfield Vogelbarke in Mycenaean pottery dates even later – Late Helladic III C (Matthäus, 1980); an Urnfield-style bird has also been recognised on a gold diadem from the citadel at Pylos (Blegen et al. 1973: 16, figure 108d; Schauer, 1986: 74).

There are also rock art representations of boats in the Aegean region, particularly those found on Cyprus at Tel Acco and at Kition-Kathari (Artzy, 2003: 232).

The Tel Acco rock carvings were found on a portable altar (and probably used on board a ship) dated to the very end of the Late Bronze Age. Similar ships are depicted at Kition, on the walls of temples I and IV, and have been interpreted as ex-voto offerings. Three other sites have produced boat rock carvings similar to those of Aegean type; these are located in Israel on the western side of the Carmel Ridge, in the Naḥal ha-Me'arot and Naḥal Oren areas (Artzy, 2003: 237), and have been dated to the Late Bronze Age IIb (Artzy, 2003: 244). The area was frequentted by Canaanite, Syrian, Cypriot, Anatolian, and Aegean merchants. Several boats are depicted on the 'pyramid' rock (a natural formation resembling a pyramid) at Naḥal ha-Me'arot, and all have prows facing west, towards the sea.

---

[5] Hekman (2003) reports 21 ships in his catalogue of materials from Chalandriani on Syros. Among these, 9 depict the theme of the sun, the ship, or both. Depictions of single ships (with fish on the prow) can be seen on 'frying pans' from tombs 174, 283, 289, 351, 356. The 'frying pan' from tomb 364 depicts two ships with fish on their prows. The 'frying pan' from tomb 322 depicts a ship with the sun, in a composition reminiscent of the Nebra Disc. 'Frying pans' from tomb 172, and one from the American School of Classical Studies at Athens (Hekman 2003, 379, figure 880), possibly depict the sun.

Dated to the very end of Late Bronze Age and Early Iron Age[6] are bronze (and copper) ship models from Sardinia, confirming that ship iconography spread vigorously and widely from the end of the Late Bronze Age and during the Early Iron Age. Migrating people may have contributed significantly in spreading and amalgamating similar ideas and developing common traits. These people, and their ideas, were undoubtedly spread over a wide area, and rapidly, thanks to the established exchange networks that developed during the Late Bronze Age.

NORTHERN EUROPE

Three main regions can be recognised in northern Europe: Scandinavia[7], Denmark, and Germany. Thousands of rock carvings, many representing ships, have been found in Scandinavia and date from Period I onwards[8]: bronzes, however, are rare. In Denmark 419 ships are represented on 419 bronze objects; a few are also found on rock. In Germany about 100 ships are depicted on bronze objects, but none on rock (Kaul, 1998: 113–117). Boat-shaped graves are found in all areas and date from Period III (Kaul, 1998: 48), although the monumental burial at Kivik (Randsborg, 1993), with several slabs depicting ships and other scenes, suggests that by Period II there was an established ship iconography connected with funerary rituals. The earliest representation has been dated to the middle of Period I (Early Bronze Age)[9], and is found on the Rørby sword (Kaul, 1998: 73–86). This peculiar type of sword (of probable indigenous manufacture) imitates the shape of a ship[10], and a representation of a ship, in the style of the earliest examples of Scandinavian rock art, is incised upon it. Kaul (1998: 75) suggests that 'the ship on the Rørby sword and the demonstration that it has close counterparts in the rock carvings show (...) that the ship was an important religious symbol in Scandinavia' long before foreign influences from the south made themselves felt. In his opinion, ships to be 'regarded as a symbol started with the beginning of the Bronze Age and the onset of the importation of larger quantities of bronze' (Kaul, 1998: 84). In other words, the ship originally symbolized wealth and therefore social power, and in the early representa-tions of ships human figures are seldom present because the focus was on the ship itself.

In contemporary central Europe, the iconography of the ship was also gaining importance – as part of a sophisticated astronomical and cosmological system. This is evident from the Nebra Disc (Figure 4.4), found[11] in Germany with an assemblage of Period I swords (Meller 2004).

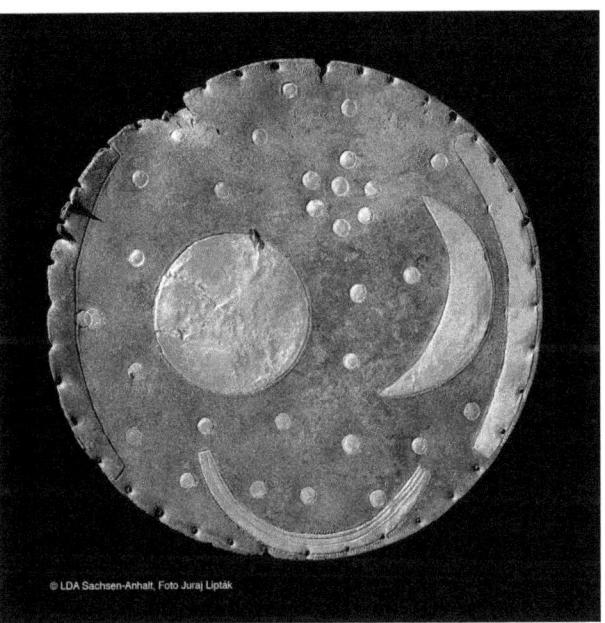

Fig. 4.4. Nebra disk, © Landesamt für Denkmalpflege und Archäologie Sachsen-Anhalt, phtograph by Juraj Lipták.

Kaul (1998) observes a surge in the iconography from Period IV (Late Bronze Age[12]), after a decrease in ship representations in Period III. By then the ship motif appears to have become associated with the theme of death[13] in Scandinavian rock art. Kaul (1998; 2005) has recognised in Danish bronzes a complex cosmology centred on the sun, borne by a ship and in the company of creatures such as the horse, snake, and fish. Some elements of this cosmology may have reached northern Europe from the central zone, and appear to have been adapted in each region and period. The arrival of the cosmology and belief system in northern Europe at the end of the Late Bronze Age would have affected the expression of pre-existing beliefs and reinvigorated the practice of representing ships in ritual contexts. It is at this point (Period IV) that performances aboard ships begin appearing on bronze representations, and, especially, on rock art. While a Hungarian influence can be recognised on bronze depictions, the rock art remains largely unaffected (Kniep, 1999). However, as we have seen, the spatial distribution of the two forms of ritual art only marginally overlaps. In the Mediterranean region, the evidence for rites taking place on board is also limited to the very end of the Late Bronze Age – corresponding to the end of Period III in northern Europe – for example the portable altar found at Tel Acco, Cyprus: the ship becomes a sacred space.

---

[6] No secure archaeological dating has been possible for any of the surviving models (Tiboni 2006, 141).

[7] Norway and Sweden.

[8] As no direct dates can be determined, rock art is dated by comparisons to styles of dated depictions on bronze artefacts.

[9] Middle Period I is dated around 1600–1500 BC.

[10] Razors imitating shapes of ships appear in Denmark from Period II (Kaul 1998, 134).

[11] Since the Disc was recovered after looting, criticism has been expressed about its authenticity – for example by Schauer (2005).

[12] 1100–900 BC, and corresponding to the Early Iron Age in the Mediterranean.

[13] The Bronze Age seascape has been interpreted by many scholars as a liminal space between land and sky, life and death (Bradley 1997; Goldhahn 1999; Van de Noort 2003; Chapman and Gearey 2004; Clark 2004; Westerdahl 2005). However this hypothesis puts the emphasis on the crew, who were often indistinct in early depictions. See also Lindenlauf (2003) for a similar interpretation of Homeric and later Greece.

Kaul (1998: 113) recognises that representations on bronzes often form 'cohesive scenes', where a number of symbols is aggregated, and he demonstrates that the scenes can be read by interpreting the ship as the focal point. He (ibid., 265) also suggests that Scandinavian rock art representations may be read in a similar way. He notices, in particular, the significance of the direction of the ships in the cosmology, derived from depictions on bronzes, and the relevance of such an observation in the interpretation of Scandinavian rock art ships. For example, all the ships in a field at Slänge are sailing towards the left; the same can be noticed in more complex scenes depicted at Fossum and Böhuslan (Kaul, 1998: 265–267). As noted above, at Naḥal ha-Me'arot, Israel, all the ships represented in the 'pyramid' were also oriented in the same direction. This opens the possibility of being able to 'read' rock art representations as coherent symbols of a language. Bouissac (1993) suggests considering the individual representations as symbols in some form of hieroglyphic writing. This hypothesis deserves some attention in the light of Kaul's successful decoding of an entire and plausible cosmology from a (largely repetitive) series of depictions on bronzes.

CONCLUSIONS

The discovery of rock art rock carvings near Gobustan has yielded the earliest and most comprehensive repertoire of ship depictions and associated symbols. It appears that the site was a ritual centre from its beginning, and, most importantly, it was connected to the Mediterranean and continental Europe. It probably took millennia for that repertoire and set of beliefs to develop, and the example from third-millennium Egypt demonstrates that, even though powerful, those cultural influences were also slow to spread.

The rock carvings near Gobustan depict a real landscape that could be easily recognised and adapted by any culture, and this was essential to their success. In Egypt ships were singled out because they symbolized royal power. It is probable that larger ships and their contents were controlled by the pharaoh, and therefore ships were equated with exceptional wealth[14]. In the same way, ships in northern Europe were probably associated with the wealth generated by exchanges of bronze. The two cultural traditions emerged independently, but they were based on the same economic reasoning. In all cases it is possible that the artistic repertoire originated from the same source – Gobustan. From there the repertoire may have spread to Greece via the Near East and into northern Europe (via central Europe). Accepting that a single repertoire was developed across millennia explains many stylistic similarities, while local adaptations would maintain the artistic and cultural independence of the adoptive regions.

During the latest phases of the Bronze Age, the transmission of both artistic style, and associated beliefs, in relation to representations of ships, changes dramatically. By then, an extensive exchange network formed, based on enterprising seafaring, and its breadth can be easily recognised from the distribution of Mycenaean pottery in the Mediterranean (Wijngaarden, 2002). At the same time many polities disintegrated, forcing many people to migrate. The existing exchange network was apparently independent from any polity, and therefore could have survived any political change unscathed. Indeed, in such regions as Cyprus (Schreiber, 2003; Steel, 2004) or Italy (Vianello, 2005: 97–99), there are no signs of interruption in long-distance trade. The mixture of people and beliefs on board ships could have easily polarized towards communal and pre-existing beliefs, such as the cult of the sun. The ship itself would have been a powerful presence for those people – an important part of their landscape.

The horizon, depicted twice on the Nebra Disc (Figure 4.4), would also suddenly have become as important as it can be to those on a sailing ship. In short, the sun, the horizon, the sky, and the ship, all visualize the mariner's landscape. Ship symbolism was brought to the Italian peninsula, perhaps unsurprisingly, by Aegean ships. In Valcamonica ships are quite rare (Fossati, 1999), and this would have not been the case if the symbolism had travelled north or south, via the Amber Route, into the Adriatic and Aegean regions.

The cultural impulse that started in the Mediterranean also affected northern Europe, and ideas were probably spread north by merchants and the elite from Hungary to Germany, and then into Denmark and Scandinavia. The symbolism of the aquatic bird seems to be a development of that region[15], and it had barely arrived into Mycenaean Greece or the Italian peninsula by the end of the Bronze Age, by which time ship symbolism was already established in those regions (Figure 4.5). The symbolism of the horse and 'wheel cross' seem, instead, to have developed in the Near East[16] and reached the Aegean and northern Europe by different routes.

The ship also became a ritual space, with ritual performances taking place on board, both in the Mediterranean (portable altars) and northern Europe (rock art depictions). During the Mediterranean Iron Age and Nordic Late Bronze Age, Period V, there is evidence of direct influences from the Mediterranean finding their way into northern Europe (Kaul, 2004: 132–133), but these are late and follow the early influences from eastern Europe. The artistic repertoire and belief system that originated in Gobustan by then had had a bearing on

---

[14] Jackson (2005) focuses on glass making in ancient Egypt and demonstrates how several centres of production, spread across the kingdom, were used in the production of a single commodity under the tight control of the Egyptian elite.

[15] Gergova (1989, 232) reports of clay double axes, boats, thrones, anthropomorphic female figurines, clay models of chariots driven by swans from tombs in the Late Bronze Age cemetery of Orsoya, Bulgaria (Thrace), and sun symbols in the earthenware of that culture.

[16] Crouwel (2005) discusses the arrival at Mycenae, during Late Helladic I, of the 'wheel cross' and the chariot from the Levant, via Crete. Randsborg (1993) recognizes influences from the Near East, and especially the Aegean, in the monument at Kivik.

Fig. 4.5. Map showing the area of cultural exchange of the aquatic bird symbol, Hungary is on the top, Transylvania (2) was a probable area of intercultural exchanges, Orsoya (1) in Thrace, where the aquatic bird appear in Late Bronze Age contexts, and northern Greece (2), where exchanges between Mycenaeans, Thracians and Transylvanians took place. © Microsoft Corporation, © NAVTEQ, © NASA (satellite photograph).

several cultural traditions, after circulating through the Bronze Age exchange networks, and a new cycle of cultural influences began during the Iron Age.

References

ANATI, E. (2001) - *Gobustan, Azerbaijan*. Capo di Ponte: Edizioni del Centro.

ARTZY, M. (2003) - Mariners and their boats at the end of the Late Bronze and the beginning of the Iron Age in the eastern Mediterranean. *Tel Aviv*. 30, p. 232-246.

BLEGEN, C. W., et al. (1973) - *The Palace of Nestor at Pylos in Western Messenia*. University Cincinnati/ Princeton University Press.

BOUISSAC, P. (1993) - Beyond style: Steps towards a semiotic hypothesis. In BAHN P.; LORBLANCHET, M. (Eds.) *Rock art studies: the post-stylistic era or where do we go from here?* Oxford: Oxbow Books. p. 203-206.

BRADLEY, R. (1997) - Death by water: boats and footprints in the rock art of western Sweden. *Oxford Journal of Archaeology*. Oxford. 16, p. 315-324.

BRADLEY, R. (2006) - Danish razors and Swedish rocks Cosmology and the Bronze Age landscape. *Antiquity*. 80, p. 372-389.

BREDHOLT CHRISTENSEN, L.; WARBURTON, D. A. (2004) - The Problem with Symbolism: Symbols for them, Symbols for us? *Semioticon*. [Accessed on 30 August 2006] Available at: http://www.semioticon. com/virtuals/symbolicity/symbol.html

CHAPMAN, H. P.; GEAREY, B. R. (2003) - The social context of seafaring in the Bronze Age revisited. *World Archaeology*. London. 36, p. 452-458.

CIALOWICZ, K. M. (1998) - Once More the Hierakonpolis Wall Painting. In Eyre, C. J. (Ed.) *Proceedings of the Seventh International Congress of Egyptologists* Leuven: Peeters, p. 273-279.

CLARK, P. (2004) - *The Dover Bronze age boat*. Swindon: English Heritage.

CROUWEL, J. (2005) - Early Chariots in the Aegean and Their Eastern Connections. In Laffineur, R.; Greco, E. (Eds.) *Emporia: Aegeans in the central and eastern Mediterranean*. Liège: Université de Liège, p. 39-44.

DAVIS, J. L. (1992) - Review of Aegean Prehistory I: The Islands of the Aegean. *American Journal of Archaeology*. 96, p. 699-756.

FARAJOVA, M. (2004) - *The images of Boats in Rock Art of Azerbaijan*. Paper read at the RASI 2004 International Rock Art Congress, Agra-Bhopal, India, 28 November - 02 December 2004.

FORMOZOV, A. A. (1980) - *Pamiatniki pervobytnogo iskusstva na territorii SSSR*. Moskva: Nauka.

FOSSATI, A. (1999) - Figures of boat in the rock art of Valcamonica. *Tracce*. [Accessed on 30 August 2006] Available at: http://www.rupestre.net/tracce/boatval.html

GERGOVA, D. (1989) - Thracian Burial Rites of Late Bronze and Early Iron Age. In *Thracians and Mycenaeans*. Leiden: Brill, p. 231-240.

GOLDHAHN, J. (1999) - Rock art and the materialisation of a cosmology. In GOLDHAHN, J. (Ed.) *Rock Art as Social Representation*. Oxford: p. 77-100.

GRAJETZKI, W. (2003) - *Burial customs in ancient Egypt: life in death for rich and poor*. London: Duckworth.

HEKMAN, J. J. (2003) - The Early Bronze Age cemetery at Chalandriani on Syros (Cyclades, Greece). Groningen: Rijksuniversiteit Groningen.

HILLER, S. (1972) - Fisch oder Schiff: Zu einem bemalten mittelbronzezeitlichen Gefassfragment aus Ägina. *Pantheon*. 30, p. 439-446.

JACKSON, C. M. (2005) - ARCHAEOLOGY: Glassmaking in Bronze-Age Egypt. *Science*. 308, p. 1750-1752.

KAUL, F. (1998) - *Ships on bronzes: a study in Bronze Age religion and iconography*. Copenhagen: Nationalmuseet.

KAUL, F. (2004) - Social and religious perceptions of the ship in Bronze Age Northern Europe. In Clark, P. (Ed.) *The Dover Bronze Age Boat in Context*. Oxford: Oxbow Books. p. 122-137.

KAUL, F. (2005) - Bronze Age tripartite cosmologies. *Praehistorische Zeitschrift*. 80, p. 135-148.

KNIEP, K. (1999) - Sonnenbarke oder Totenschiff. Überlegungen zur Bedeutung der Schiffsdarstellungen auf den bronzezeitlichen Felsbildern Südskandinaviens *Deutsches Schiffahrtsarchiv*. 22, p. 247-264.

KRISTIANSEN, K. (2004) - Sea faring voyages and rock art ships. In Clark, P. (Ed.) *The Dover Bronze Age Boat in Context*. Oxford: Oxbow Books. p. 111-121.

KRISTIANSEN, K.; LARSSON, T. B. (2005) - *The rise of Bronze Age society: travels, transmissions and transformations*. Cambridge: Cambridge University Press.

LINDENLAUF, A. (2003) - The sea as a place of no return in ancient Greece. *World Archaeology*. 35, p. 416-433.

MATTHÄUS, H. (1980) - Mykenische Vogelbarken: Antithetische Tierprotomen in der Kunst des östlichen Mittelmeeraumes. *Archäologisches Korrespondenzblatt*. 10, p. 319-330.

MCCAULEY, R. N.; LAWSON, E. T. (2002) - *Bringing ritual to mind: psychological foundations of cultural forms*. Cambridge: Cambridge University Press.

MCGRAIL, S. (2003) - The sea and archaeology. *Historical Research*. 76, p. 1-17.

MELLER, H. (2004) - *Der geschmiedete Himmel: die weite Welt im Herzen Europas vor 3600 Jahren*. Stuttgart: Theiss.

MERCER, S. A. B. (1952) - *The Pyramid Texts in Translation and Commentary*. New York: Longmans, Green & Co.

RANDSBORG, K. (1993) - *Kivik: archaeology & iconography*. Kobenhavn: Munksgaard.

RUTTER, J. B. (1993) - Review of Aegean Prehistory II: The Prepalatial Bronze Age of the Southern and Central Greek Mainland. *American Journal of Archaeology*. 97, p. 745-797.

SCHAUER, P. (1986) - *Goldkegel der Bronzezeit. Ein Beitrag zur Kulturverbindung zwischen Orient und Mitteleuropa*. Mainz: Römisch-Germanischen Zentralmuseums Mainz.

SCHAUER, P. (2005) - Kritische Anmerkungen zum Bronzeensemble mit "Himmelsscheibe" Angeblich vom Mittelberg bei Nebra, Sachsen-Anhalt. *Archäologisches Korrespondenzblatt*. 35, p. 323-328.

SCHREIBER, N. (2003) - *The Cypro-Phoenician pottery of the Iron Age*. Leiden; Boston: Brill. (Culture and history of the ancient Near East; 13).

SIEDENTOPF, H. B. (1991) - *Mattbemalte Keramik der mittleren Bronzezeit*. Mainz/Rhein: Zabern. (Alt-Ägina; IV, 2).

STEEL, L. (2004) - *Cyprus before history: from the earliest settlers to the end of the Bronze Age*. London: Duckworth.

TIBONI, F. (2006) - Animal-Shaped Figureheads and the Evolution of a 'Keel-Post-Stem' Structure in Nuragic Bronze Models and Boats between the 9th and 7th Centuries BC. *The International Journal of Nautical Archaeology*. 35, p. 141-144.

VAN DE NOORT, R. (2003) - An ancient seascape: the social context of seafaring in the early Bronze Age. *World Archaeology*. London. 35, p. 404-415.

VERNER, M. (2002) - *The pyramids: their archaeology and history*. London: Atlantic Books.

VIANELLO, A. (2005) - *Late Bronze Age Mycenaean and Italic products in the West Mediterranean: a social and economic analysis*. BAR Publishing

WACHSMANN, S. (2000) - To the Sea of the Philistines. In Oren, E. D. (Ed.) *The Sea Peoples and Their World: A Reassessment*. Philadelphia: The University Museum, University of Pennsylvania. p. 103-143.

WARD, C. (2006) - Boat-building and its social context in early Egypt: interpretations from the First Dynasty boat-grave cemetery at Abydos. *Antiquity*. 80, p. 118-129.

WESTERDAHL, C. (2005) - Seal on Land, Elk at Sea: Notes on and Applications of the Ritual Landscape at the Seaboard. *The International Journal of Nautical Archaeology*. 34, p. 2-23.

WILKINSON, T. A. H. (1999) - *Early Dynastic Egypt*. London, New York: Routledge.

WIJNGAARDEN, G. J. V. (2002) - *Use and appreciation of Mycenaean pottery in the Levant, Cyprus and Italy (1600-1200 B.C.)*. Amsterdam: Amsterdam University Press.

WILLIAMS, B. (1988) - *Decorated Pottery and the Art of Naquada III*. Munich: Deutscher Kunstverlag.

COGNITIVE ARCHAEOLOGY, ROCK ART AND ARCHAEOASTRONOMY: INTERRELATED DISCIPLINES

Fernando Augusto COIMBRA

Institute Land and Memory – Center for Superior Studies (Mação, Portugal)

Abstract: The subject of cognitive archaeology is to study the ways of past thought, trough material remains. This way, rock art is a privileged field for doing that, because it allows the contact with "images from ancient worlds as ancient human minds envisioned them" (Taçon, Chippindale, 1998). As one can see, rock art has a kind of "directness", since the engravings are "direct material expressions of human concepts, of human thought" (Idem, Ibidem). On another hand, archaeoastronomy interlerrates with cognitive archaeology, because it studies early cognitive abilities from past civilizations. It also interrelates with rock art, because, in some cases, it may explain some engravings not understood by only archaeologists. Rock art interrelates with archaeastronomy, since some engraved or painted rocks depict celestial environments and also astronomical transitory phenomena like comets.

In this paper, the author presents some theoretical considerations, regarding the interrrelationship of the three mentioned disciplines, that will be illustrated with examples of rock art from different parts of the world. This way, studying rock art with the contributes of cognitive archaeology and archaeoastronomy, it will lead to a research about symbolic archaeology done with a scientific approach.

Keywords: Cognitive archaeology, rock art, archaeoastronomy, past thought.

Résumé : Le sujet de l' archeologie cognitive est l' étude des formes de la pensée du passé, à travers des vestiges matériaux. De cette façon, l' art rupestre est un champ privilégié pour le faire, parce qu' elle permet un contact avec "images from ancient worlds as ancient human minds envisioned them" (Taçon, Chippindale, 1998). Comme on peut observer, l' art rupestre a un caractère direct, une fois que les gravures sont "direct material expressions of human concepts, of human thought" (IDEM). Dans un autre côté, l' archeoastronomie se relacione avec l' archeologie cognitive, parce qu' elle étudie dés capacités cognitives primitives de civilizations disparues. Elle se realacione aussi avec l' art rupestre, parce que, en quelques examples, elle peut expliquer des gravures non comprises par seulement des archeólogues. L' art rupestre se relacione avec l' archeoastronomie, une fois que quelques rochers peints ou gravés réprésentent des ambiants celestes et aussi des phénomènes astronomiques transitoires comme des comètes.

Dans cet article l' auteur presente de quelques considérations théoriques relatives à les interrelations entre les trois disciplines indiquées, qui seront illustrées avec des examples de l' art rupestre de diverses régions du monde. De cette façon, étudiant l' art rupestre avec les contributs de l' archeologie cognitive et de l' archeoastronomie aportera a une recherche sur l' archeologie symbolique efectuée avec une méthode scientifique.

Mots clés: Archeologie cognitive, art rupestre, archeoastronomie, pensée passée

INTRODUCTORY NOTE

This paper is the result of some reflexions upon cognitive archaeology, rock art, archaeoastronomy and the possible relations between them. It's mainly theoretical, but is also illustrated with some specific examples. But, first of all, it's necessary to make some brief considerations about the aims of these three disciplines, in order to understand what are we talking about.

The subject of cognitive archaeology is "the study of past ways of thought, as inferred from material remains" (Renfrew, 1994a: 3). Cognitive archaeology is one of the newest branches of modern archaeology. It's an archaeology of the mind.

Rock art is a discipline that studies carvings and paintings on rock surfaces, since the Paleolithic untill recent times. Of course there are several kinds of approaches to rock art studies, according to the different researchers all over the world, since rock art is a world wide phenomenon.

Archaeoastronomy studies cognitive astronomical abilities from past civilizations. Some archaeologists are still not very fond of this discipline, because in its beginnings some researchers were non-scientific, using very ambiguous and subjective approaches. But, today, several archaeoastronomers have a true scientific method in their survey, and, for example, at Leicester University there's a recent graduation on Archaeoastronomy. Furthermore, in the 90's, an interdisciplinary team of archaeologists and astronomers studied more than three hundred dolmen in the Iberian Peninsula, from the North to the South, and concluded that only 3% were turned to the sunrise at any time of the year (Belmonte Avilés, 1999). Let's refer that, not so long ago, there was the "archaeological myth" that almost all these megalithic monuments were aligned with the sunrise due to funerary rituals. This way one can begin to understand the importance of archaeoastronomy for archaeological research.

But let's start to analyze the relation between these mentioned disciplines:

COGNITIVE ARCHAEOLOGY AND ROCK ART

Rock art is a privileged field for studying past ways of thought, because it allows the contact with "images from ancient worlds as ancient human minds envisioned them" (Taçon; Chippindale, 1998: 2). It has a kind of "direct-

Fig. 5.1. Inscription with a swastika used as a letter.

ness", since the engravings are "direct material expressions of human concepts, of human thought" (idem, ibidem: 2). Rock art can tell many things about the past ways of thought and habits. It can inform us about ritual and mythology. It can tell also about the kind of houses, clothes, weapons and other artefacts used by our ancestrors, some of these also used in a symbolic way. It can be considered as the oldest archive of Mankind. According to Dario Seglie, rock art is the "oldest trace of human spirituality" and "constitutes an inalienable patrimony relative to the Original Thought of Man" (Seglie, 1999: 12).

Several researchers approach rock art studies with a semiotic perspective, "developing new perspectives on the archaeology of writting systems and the evolution of humans cognitive and communicative functions" (Bouissac; Khan, 1995: 49). Indeed, in a great deal of examples of engravings seems to exist a "code" transmited along the generations. For example, in the Rock of the Signs (Barcelos, Portugal) the different carvings of the main pannel are organized in a circular way, leaving a circular empty space in the middle of them, seeming to have been made according to a certain "grammar" or even "semantics" (Coimbra, 2004). Regarding the evolution of the writting systems and the human communicative abilities, an inscription on a rock known as Laje da Fechadura (Sertã, Portugal), shows the association of alphabethic letters and a swastika, motif that certainly represents some concept, some idea, depicted by a symbol instead by letters (Fig. 5.1).

Today is usually assumed that rock art has, most of the times, a symbolic religious character. This way it seems a better field for a cognitive archaeological approach than the research, for example, of themes like pottery, sculpture, or architecture, although symbolic they may be. However, some rock art studies about symbolism are too much subjective and lack of an objective methodology. But with cognitive processual archaeology this problem can be solved. According to Colin Renfrew, "the task for the cognitive archaeologist is to devise methods of study (...) wich will, in practice, allow the archaeological evidence to be used to make contributions to the discussion wich goes beyond more general speculation" (Renfrew, 1994a: 5). The same author also refers that "an important component of the cognitive-processual approach is (...) to examine the ways in wich symbols were used. This may be contrasted with the attempt to seek rather to ascertain their meaning" (idem, ibidem: 6).

These last ideas have been very useful in our own research about rock art symbolism. For example, we've been studying the pentagram in rock art for several years[1] and noticed that a good method is to see, first of all, how the symbol is used, instead of trying to get a meaning for it. It's also important to understand the context in wich the symbol appears. These procedures will lead to an interpretation that can be considered with an objective character, instead of subjective.

COGNITIVE ARCHAEOLOGY AND ARCHAEOASTRONOMY

Archaeoastronomy interelates with cognitive archaeology, because it studies astronomical cognitive abilities from past civilizations and what those peoples thought about the celestial phenomena. It must be stressed that comets were allready noticed by early civilizations, since they are refered in inscriptions from Babylon, dated from the end of the II millenium BC. In fact, the Babylonians and the Chinese had an obssession in observing the sky. This may be related to the need of controlling the danger of astral impacts on Earth. According to Bill Napier, from Armagh Observatory, Ireland, "there are likely to have been epochs when the sky contained one or more visible,

---

[1] See our article - "Some interpretive possibilities about the pentagram in rock art", presented to the WS 34 Session on the 15th UISPP Congress.

periodic comets, associated with annual fireball storms of huge intensity (...). Such phenomena (...) surely had a profound effect on the minds of early peoples. At a minimum, traces of this ancient sky should be detectable in the artefacts and belief systems of the earliest cultures" (Napier, 1998: 31).

Some British astronomers argue that "comets and comet-related phenomena seem to have played an important part in the beliefs and social habits of most known civilizations from the very earliest times" (Bailey, *et alli*, 1990: 8). These ideas are represented in several mythologies and in the arts of very different cultures around the world.[2] For example, the myth of the birth of the goddess Athina, that comes out from Zeus' head, could have been inspired by the breaking in two of a giant comet, a phenomenon well known by astrophysicists.

Around 5500 BC a giant meteorite fell on Kaali, in Saareema island near Estonia, provoking great destruction and a large crater where later a lake was formed. Near this place there were found archaeological evidences of gifts, since early times, being, this way, the site probably considered sacred. Curiously, today this region is called, in Estonian, *Püha*, wich means sacred (Kaali web page).

Comets were unambiguously represented in Celtic and Roman coins, being one of these astral orbs worshiped in a temple in Rome, precisely the comet that appeared during the games dedicated to *Venus Genitrix*, after Cesar's death. The people of Rome interpreted this event as the arrival of Cesar's soul among the imortal gods.

In more recent times, the Chumash indians, from California, believed that a meteor was a person's soul on its way to the afterlife and the Wintu indians explained meteors as the spirits of shamans traveling to the Otherworld (Kronk, n/d).

Other celestial events like total eclipses must also have impressed the earliest civilizations, being represented, so it seems, in artefacts of different countries. According to Piero Barale, the ancient peoples from Center-Europe interpreted eclipses as the intention of a enormous wolf in devouring the sun or the moon. Besides some possible cases in rock art, there's an excellent unambiguous example in a Gaulish gold coin from the 1st Century BC, where a wolf, with a large open mouth, is bitting a disc placed high in the sky (Barale, 2003).

The study of past ways of human thought, related to astronomy, must also consider the work of classical writers as *Herodotus*, *Caius Plini Secundi* (Elder Pliny), *Lucius Anaeus Seneca* and *Apollonius* from Myndus, among others. For example, the first one "speaks of the tribe of the Atarantes of Lybia who cursed the sun but invoked the sky for its rain-making properties" (Green,

1991: 16). In fact, in hot and dry lands, the sun can be seen as an enemy, provoking drought and destroying agriculture. In cold, wet and dark countries, the sun can be seen as as god, warming the bodies and iluminating the day.

In spite of the scepticism among some archaeologists regarding the solar religion, megalithic sun-imagery is the first unambiguous evidence for a solar cult in Europe. According to Miranda Green, "the solar motifs engraved in passage graves could have been placed there as a comfort to the dead, as a reminder that rebirth and renewal would take place" (Green, 1991: 27).

In European Iron Age, the sun will be associated with animals as stags, horses and water birds, that become solar symbols. But this is a subject for another article and cannot be developed here, due to the limit of space. For the same reason, it's impossible to refer many examples of artefacts and mythologies with different chronologies, representing celestial events, that appear in several cultures around the world.

ROCK ART AND ARCHAEOASTRONOMY

Archaeoastronomy also interrelates with rock art, because, in some cases, it may explain some engravings not understood only by archaeologists. For example, in the Rock 35 from Foppe di Nadro (Valcamonica, Italy), the Italian astronomer Adriano Gaspani identified a represent-tation of a comet that had never been understood that way by the archaeologists that studied the site (Gaspani, n/d).

Rock art interrelates with archaeastronomy, since some engraved or painted rocks depict celestial environments and also astronomical transitory phenomena like comets and meteors. These astral orbs must have left a deep impression in the minds of the observers, due to the visual impact that they produced, being considered probably as manifestations of the gods. A good example can be seen in the *San* Rock Art from South Africa, in the Bethlehem District. It's about a painting with three anthropomorfic figures that have the arms in a position that they look like flying, being probably a ritual scene (Fig. 5.2). There's also a kind of feathers in the arms of these characters, above whom one can see the depiction of a fireball.[3]

In Mont Bego (France), there are some carvings from the III millenium BC very similar to cometary representations from the 16th century (Barale, 2003), giving the idea of dynamic movement.

---

[2] Curiously, in some cultures, comets are seen as good omens, while in others they are interpreted as bad omens.

[3] A fireball is a meteor with a luminescence equivalent to Venus, wich leave a tail visible for some minutes. The astral body that appears in this example of the San Rock Art was identified as a fireball by Tim Cooper, Director of the Comet and Meteor Section of the Astronomical Society of Southern Africa (Ouzman, in press). I thank Doctor Sven Ouzman for sending me this article even before beeing completely published.

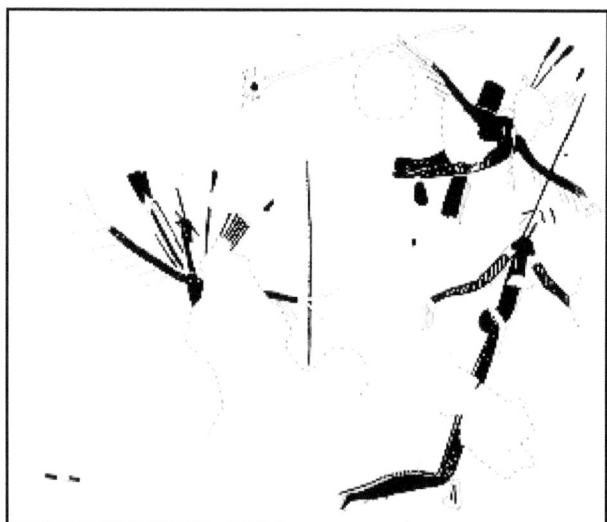

Fig. 5.2. Fireball (on the top) in *San* ritual scene. (After Ouzman).

Fig. 5.3. Rock of Botelhinha. The sunbeams enter the hole and highlight the engravings

In the end of the 20th century, Landscape Archaeology became very popular, allowing a new approach to Archaeology. Today, archaeologists must be aware that the sky, specially in certain periods of the day, is also a kind of "landscape". Let's not forget that prehistoric peoples had no calendars and needed to know what was the exact time of the year for sewing and for other agricultural works, in order to get a good harvest. Their lifes depended on that. So, they started to mark the time by the position of some astral bodies in the sky.[4] The painted rock shelter of Pala Pinta (Alijó, Vila Real, Portugal), that has beautiful astral depictions, possibly could be a calendar. It has two similar "solar motifs", in different positions but both aligned. Maybe one corresponds to the winter solstice, and the other to the summer solstice. Writting these ideas without astronomical measurements is of course speculation, but it's made here on purpose, just to show the need of an interdisciplinary survey between rock art reserchers and astronomers in cases like this one. It also shows, once more, the close relation between rock art and archaeoastronomy.

In the Rock of Botelhinha (Pegarinhos, Alijó), not far from Pala Pinta Rock Shelter, there's another good example of this relation. The rock has a strange shape and natural holes trough where the sunlight iluminates continuously several carvings (Fig. 5.3). The rock has several engravings all around it, but the main concentration is precisely in a natural hole where the sunlight slowly gets in. This is probably related with some prehistoric ritual. In fact, in Prehistory, the relation between Astronomy and Religion is very close.

In Armenia several engravings seem to depict astral orbs (Fig. 5.4), as for example at Sevsar Mountain, considered as an astronomical observatory by some Armenian resear-

Fig. 5.4. "The Astronomical Observatory", Armenia (after Martirosian, 1975).

chers. In fact, this country has a big concentration of important rock art pannels, that are not yet well known in western Europe.[5]

---

[4] Michael Rappenglüeck has been arguing that in Lascaux cave there are already calendars based on the moon (Rappenglüeck, 2000).

[5] In September 2003, during a workshop about rock art in Greece, we had the opportunity of meeting Prof. Dr. Karen Tokathyan, an Armenian astrophysicist and rock art researcher that showed us several photos of rock art from his country. Armenia has indeed a great potential in rock art that should be spread among all the researchers of this discipline.

In the Copper Age stelae from Valcamonica, Italy, the representation of the sun appears very often, usually in the top of these monuments, giving the idea of a sun-cult that, indeed, seems to spread in almost all parts of Late Prehistoric Europe.

On the rock known as *Peira Eicrita*,[6] from San Germano Chisone (Piemonte region, Italy), that was considered as a Bronze Age solar astronomical observatory (Seglie, n/d), besides other engravings one can see a swastika symbol with its cruciform structure perfectlly aligned to the North, South, East and West.

At Coll de la Font Roja (Caixás, East Pyrenees, France), there are engravings consisting in pentagrams associated with rayed motives. One of these has also a kind of a triple tail, that may be the representation of a comet. In fact, real comets show often three tails like it happens on this petroglyph.

Finally, at Dalby, Denmark, there's a rock with cup-marks pecked in a way that seem to depict groups of stars (Coimbra, 2001). Comparing those engraved motifs with real constellations the similarity is amazing.

There are many more examples, around the world, of this relation between rock art and archaeoastronomy, but we must stop by now due to the limit of pages for this article. Thus, let's finnish with some conclusions and some final statements.

CONCLUSIONS AND FINAL STATEMENTS

Since Prehistory, Man made signs on cave walls, on ceramics and on other materials. And even before knowing writing, Man carved "messages" and registered several events on rocks, using both symbols and natural images. This way, rock art can be considered as the oldest archive of Mankind and it's surely a priceless record of past events, allowing us to know directlly, nowadays, many information[7] from the past (Coimbra, in press). Rock art is a pivileged field of research for cognitive archaeology, because it allows a "direct" contact with the minds of our ancestrors and can tell many things about the past ways of thought and habits. It's also important for the study of ancient astronomical abilities, because it depicts ancient celestial environments.

On the other hand, rock art benefits from the development of Cognitive Processual Archaeology, specially as a method for studying its meannings. The idea of C. Renfrew (1994a) in examining the ways in wich symbols were used, rather than to try to decipher their significance, it's an important methodological approach, indispensable for a scientific symbolic archaeology.

The increasing studies of archaeoastronomy are also an excellent field of work for cognitive archaeology, since they deal with astronomical cognitive abilities from past civilizations and so may lead to understand what those peoples thought about the celestial phenomena. This way, archaeoastronomy may be a great help in studying ancient mythologies, because they often envolve celestial events understandable only by the development of Astronomy.

On another hand, the study of past ways of thought trough ancient iconography can provide many important information for archaeoastronomers that, unfortunatelly, many times forget this indispensable data. As we mentioned above, some engraved or painted rocks depict celestial environments and also astronomical transitory phenomena like comets and meteors. These "artistic" manifestations should be studied together by rock art researchers and by archaeoastronomers.

Let us finnish this article with an invitation to the archaeoastronomers present in this session, to come again to Portugal and study the astronomical representations on rock art, on megalithic art and on other archaeological artefacts. We are sure that everyone who comes will find an immense field of research that will be quite relevant for the future not only of cognitive archaeology but also of rock art and archaeoastronomy.

References

BAILEY, M.E.; CLUBE, S.V.M.; NAPIER, W.M. (1990) – *The origin of comets*. Oxford: Pergamon Press, p. 1-39.

BARALE, P. (2003) – *Il Cielo del popolo del Faggio: Sole, Luna e Stelle dei Ligures Bagienni*. Pollenzo: Associazione Turistica Pro Loco, p. 122-134.

BATATA, C.; COIMBRA, F. A.; GASPAR, F. (2004) – As gravuras rupestres da Laje da Fechadura (Concelho da Sertã). *Revista de Portugal, Nova Série*. V. N. de Gaia. 1, p. 26-31.

BELMONTE AVILÉS, J. A. (1999) – *As Leis do Céu. Astronomia e Civilizações Antigas*. Lisboa: Mareantes Editores, p. 11-134; p.169-287.

BOUISSAC, P; KHAN, M. (1995) – Semiotics, signs and symbols (Rationale). In *Supplemento a Survey, NEWS-95 International Rock Art Congress*. Pinerolo: Centro Studi e Museo di Arte Preistorica. p. 48-49.

COIMBRA, F. A. (2001) – The cup-marks in rock art in Western Europe. A contribute to its study and interpretation, Proceedings of the Congress "Le incisione rupestri non figurative nell'arco alpino meridionale", Museo del Paesaggio, Verbania. www.artepreistorica.it

---

[6] In the traditional local language, *Peira Eicrita* means "written rock". Variations of this name appear also, very often, in other Latin countries such as France, Spain and Portugal.

[7] For example, the engravings from the Tassili Desert, in North Africa, depicting elephants, giraffes and other animals from the Savanah, prove that this region was once fertile, providing important data for Paleoenvironmental studies.

COIMBRA, F.A. (2004) – As gravuras rupestres do concelho de Barcelos (Portugal): Subsídios para o seu estudo. *Anuário Brigantino*. Betanzos. 27, p. 37-70.

COIMBRA, F. A. (in press) – Comets and meteors in rock art: evidences and possibilities. 13th SEAC Conference Proceedings, Isili.

GASPANI, A. (n/d) – Tracce di una Cometa della Etá del Ferro sulla roccia N. 35 di Foppe di Nadro in Valcamonica. www.artepreistorica.it

GREEN, M. (1991) – *The Sun-Gods of Ancient Europe*. London: B. T.Batsford, L.td, p. 11-60; p.137-138.

KAALI WEB PAGE (n/d) – Kaali. www.muinas.ee/ecp/kaali/en/index.html

KRONK, G. W. (n/d) – Meteors and the Native Americans. www.maa.agleia.de/comet/metlegends.html

MARTIROSIAN, H. A. (1975) – *The rock carvings of the Gegham Mountain Range*. Yerevan: Academy of Science of Armenia.

NAPIER, W.M. (1998) – Cometary catastrophes, cosmic dust and ecological disasters in historical times: the astronomical framework. In PEISER, B. J.; PALMER, T.; BAILEY, M. E. eds. *Natural catastrophes during Bronze Age civilisations: archaeological, geological, astronomical and cultural perspectives*. Oxford: B. A. R., p. 21-32. (BAR International Series, 728).

OUZMAN, S. (in press) – Flashes of brilliance: San rock paintings of Heaven's Things. In *Lewis-Williams meeting book*.

RAPPENGLÜECK, M. (2000) – Ice Age star map discovered. http://news.bbc.co.uk/1/hi/sci/tech/871930.stm

RENFREW, C. (1994a) – Towards a cognitive archaeology. In *The ancient mind*. Cambridge: Cambridge University Press. p. 3-12.

RENFREW, C. (1994b) – The archaeology of religion. In *The ancient mind*. Cambridge: Cambridge University Press. p. 47-54.

RENFREW, C.; BAHN, P. (1993) – *Arqueologia. Teorias, Métodos y Práctica*. Madrid: Ediciones Akal, S. A. p. 355-387; p. 425-455.

SEGLIE, D. (1995) – Opening address. News 95 International Rock Art Congress. In *Supplemento a Survey. News 95 International Rock Art Congress*. Pinerolo: Centro Studi e Museo di Arte Preistorica, p. 11-13.

SEGLIE, D. (n/d) – La "Peira Eicrita" de San Germano Chisone, Italie. www.cesmap.it

TAÇON, P.; e CHIPPINDALE, C. (1998) – An archaeology of rock-art through informed methods and formal methods. In *The Archaeology of Rock Art*. Cambridge: Cambridge University Press, p. 1-10.

SPACE SYNTAX ANALYSIS AS COGNITIVE APPROACH TO PREHISTORIC MENTALITY

George DIMITRIADIS

Hellenic Rock Art Centre, Philippi-Greece, g.dimitriadis@herac.gr
International Summer School European Prehistory, Sardinia, Italy, issep@cheapnet.it

Abstract: The author is convinced that Space is more important as human existence parameter than Time. Starting point to this cognitive approach to the prehistoric mentality is the space syntax analysis of the various archaeological evidences in different scales. The anthropomorphic territory as expression of the dispositional collocation of tribal dwellings and the figurative composition on megalithic slabs are two different scale examples how prehistoric humans tried to re-organize space according to their mentality.
Keywords: cognitive archaeology, figurative composition, prehistoric mentality, space syntax analysis.

Résumé : L'auteur est convaincu que l'Espace est plus important comme un paramètre de l'existence humaine que le Temps. Le point de départ pour cette approche cognitive à la mentalité préhistorique c'est l'analyse de la syntaxe de l'espace des diverses évidences archéologiques en échelles différentes. Le territoire anthropomorphique comme expression de la colocation dépositional des habitations tribales et la composition figurative dans des étais mégalithiques sont deux exemples d'échelle différentes comme l'homme préhistorique a tenté de réorganiser l'espace d' après sa mentalité.
Mots-clés : Archéologie cognitive, composition figurative, mentalité préhistorique, analyse de la syntaxe de l'espace.

INTRODUCTION: A BRIEF HISTORY OF SPACESCAPE, TIMESCALES AND ARCHAEOLOGICAL RECORD

Reading the archaeological literature, it becomes apparent that the most important variables (quanta) are: spacescape, timescales and formation of archaeological record.

Lucien Febvre and Mark Bloch were the two prominent founders of the *Annales* School in the late 1920s applying a deep, permanent and new approach to think the historical process. They suggested that history is not a simple time sequence of events, but its formation is based on a bipolar system, continuity/change plenty of social tensions (Bloch, 1954). *Annales* School was also the principal inspiration for theoretical archaeologists during the late 1980s and early 1990s (Hodder, 1987; Bintliff, 1991; Knapp, 1992; Gurevich, 1995). Their ideas were developed on a cyclical pattern of history as Cobb (1991) model predict: repetitive short circuits which embody local fluctuations of historical events.

Besides, in late 1940s by Richardson and Kroeber (1952) another historical approach was developed independently sharing the ideas of post-Newtonian science and non linear dynamics. History was perceived as a living system characterized by traits of continuity-discontinuity rather than a system in equilibrium (Renfrew and Cook, 1979; Friedman, 1982). The emerging element is rapid transformation.

The latest attempts to describe efficiently history were the application of catastrophe theories developed by Thom (1972) in natural science from one side and chaos and thermodynamic theories proposed to physical sciences by Prigogine and Stengers (1984). In both theoretical approaches the core idea is the rate of change or the differentiation in scale (McGlade, 1987, 1999; Van der Leeuw and McGlad, 1997). Summarizing on this development we can assert that all the approaches share time conception in terms of tension otherwise as dynamicity.

During the same period -late 1980s- in North America the theoretical debate was too hard regarding the "nature" of the archaeological record. In particular the attention was to establish the formation process. Two were the main promoters for such scientific debate: Lewis Binford (1981) who promoted the idea of the archaeological process as a frozen record of a living cultural system at one particular moment of the past; and Michael Schiffer (1976), who promoted clear distinction between archaeological context (i.e. archaeological site) and the systemic context (past cultural system of the same archaeological site in examination), which embodies the archaeological context through an ongoing process called *transforms*. Binford's theory described the archaeological evidences as *dynamic* meanwhile Schiffer described it fossil.

Where does the truth stand? Each and every archaeological record belongs to the whole of before it is unearthed. Of course it was "burnt" as fossil in a particular moment but it's life continue.

> Stonehenge is not just a prehistoric monument – it is also a Roman one, a Medieval one and a contemporary one, no matter whether it has been physically intervened with or not (Thomas, 1996: 62-3).

This means that the archaeological record is inactive because buried but continues to part of the landscape or spacescape and the natural processes. Standing from that viewpoint, the spacescape permits us to distinguish the duration of the depositional process in archaeological sites (Lucas, 2005: 40).

> [...] objects have a cultural history (Lucas, 2005: 56).

Thus, speaking about time and space in archaeology is more complex because cultural history implies social memory. Time depends on space scale (topology) and spacescape (society) modifications in time (Harris, 1989). Indeed, Mizoguchis' (1993) researches remark that social memory is relative to burial modalities (*who, where and what*). Seasonal patterns of agriculture also denote the prehistoric mentality. The time is revealed throughout space elements (i.e. burial rituals in houses or seals and other artefacts designate a cyclical conception of time, cf. Bailey, 1993; Dimitriadis, 2006). Time becomes intelligible and imaginable thanks to spatial notations.

OVERVIEW ON LANDSCAPE: A PHILOSOPHICAL APPROACH

We have seen how time is perceived through a spacescape. Now its time to define how spacescape fits within the human condition and how it transforms the environment and landscape. Human conditions can be translated as human body and human body is extension of materiality and materiality remain permanently open to humans –hosting existence questions about *Being* and *be* (cf. Dimitriadis, 2006a) because landscape mark bodies: these bodies can be viewed submerged in the *wilderness* landscape.

We need to explore now how wilderness condition transform human consciousness in *wildness*? Wildness corresponds to a set of possibilities laying unexplored on the landscape. This mean that humans perceived the environment (containing more landscapes) and landscape (built up as the annihilation of more than one places) according their own culture view. Indeed, as Nash quotes:

> wilderness is a question of perception, part of mind geography (1982: 333).

Natural landscape *equals* human landscape. A *sine qua non* condition that humanity shares with the animal world. Animals live *in* their natural environment; humans live *on* the their constructed spacescape. This condition is not so obvious: humanity is permanently developing an *environmental literacy*, which is a critical point in our own evolutionary process. How we shall manage our relation with Nature and our human nature? What kind of configuration could be imprinted on the core of the landscape called Place? How we shall read the place? There is a pre-constitute pattern or what else?

Some historical remarks on Space Syntax Analysis (SSA)

From the moment that the space around the body has a consistence then things can be seen from a current vantage point. So, human activity takes place in space and is represented by spatial relations and viewpoints. Indeed, human constructed landscapes are organized around salient landmarks. Which is the hidden mentality[1] in those spatial constructs? Tversky (1993) speaks about "cognitive collage". What order I must follow to read it? The answer is space syntax analysis (SSA).

The term **space syntax** encompasses a set of theories and techniques for the analysis of spatial configurations. Hillier and Leaman (1975) and Hillier *et alii* (1976) use the term "syntax" to refer to rules that account for the generation of elementary, but fundamentally different, spatial arrangements. Hillier and Hanson (1984) define syntaxes as combinatorial structures which order the world and also allow us to retrieve descriptions of it. Hillier *et alii* (1983) and Hillier et al (1987) define "space syntax" as a methodology or a set of techniques for the representation, quantification, and interpretation of spatial configuration in buildings and settlements (Peponis *et alii* 1997).

The general idea is that spaces can be broken down into components, analyzed as networks of choices, then represented as maps and graphs that describe the relative connectivity and integration of those spaces. It rests on three basic conceptions of space:

1. *visibility polygon* (or viewshed): the field of view from any particular point, called *isovist* by Benedikt (1979).

2. straight sight-line and possible path: named *axial space* by Bill Hillier (1996). Axial lines are used in space syntax to simplify connections between spaces that make up an urban or architectural morphology.

3. imagined as a wireframe diagram: no line between two of its points goes outside its perimeter defined as *convex space* by John Peponis (1997).

FEW ANNOTATIONS ON PREHISTORIC MENTALITY FROM A SSA VIEWPOINT

I approach prehistoric mentality according a new methodological approach which is the so-called bilogic model (Dimitriadis, forthcoming). It consists in a micro-thematic analysis strategy (m-TAS) in order to capture the logic of the ancient artists during their engraved figure activity. Indeed, this task (m-TAS) serves to develop a methodological and epistemological architecture frame on prehistoric art. I accept the following model by Hofstadter (1979: 73) in which all the levels of the system *mind/prehistoric art* are connected. Their connection is structured in order to raise the imagination to the state of a hologram, i.e. to apply *a geographic map of possibility of the stratigraphic synthesis*; an isomorphic transformation of paintings and prehistoric recordings.

---

[1] In archaeological literature it is also used the term Structure of Mental Spaces (cf. Tversky, 2001).

I spoke about geographic possibilities as keywords for a cognitive approach to understand space. But space is shaped as expression of social human behaviour and in extension

> social spatiality could be simultaneously real and imagined. It functions as form, configured materially as things in space as well as mentally as thoughts about space; but also as process as a dynamic force that it always actively being produced and reproduced (Soja, 2001).

A tentative answer could come out from some math models applied on prehistoric sites.

A CONCISE SSA APPLICATIONS IN PREHISTORY: GRAVITY, GRID AND DIFFUSION MODELS[2]

Trough spacescape perception it is possible to use math models to analyze "valuation" term. The resulting values by such "estimation" could mark out the "social logic" (Soja, 2001) embodied in a landmarks system (Dalton & Banfa, 2003).

Considering the different "culture attractors" presented on the ground, it could be possible to recognize such "nodal regions" which define in unequivocal way the potentiality of an area as coming out by the "space potential" concept.

The influence of a given data Ai on just any j is expressed:

(1) $\quad I = PAi / Dij^{a}$ [Morrill]

[PAi express the "potentiality" of the point Ai; Dij equal to the distance between the two points; ^{a} indicate an exponent of the formula which adapt the formula in every real situation].

Obviously the total potential of the data Aj is equal to the summary of the single potential and is given by the formula:

(2) $\quad IAi = k$

[k formula's adaptation costant].

The concept of "nodal region" permit to configure better the concept of "grid" or "web"[3] defined as the "flux of (...)" persons, goods, ideas etc. Indeed, according Lynch's (1960: 67) syntactical interpretation of the space elements it is possible to distinguish a first order of elements including:

1. *Paths* conceived as channels for potential movement similar to the axial concept of Hiller;
2. *Nodes* considered as key points which crucial route choises are offered and characterized by a strong visual identity;
3. *Districts* assembled in order to collect the stratify inherent sense of the place.

The problem is now to attempt the understanding of the complex structure of the territory. How is it possible to bridge between "nodal regions" and "cultural attractors"[4]?

The "edge" definition to isovist space may provide an answer: *visual prominent boundary* or as "catchment area" generating by the districts (Peponis *et alii*, 1998).

Another solution could be the gradient of space diffusion of the innovation as integrated part of Hägerstrand protocol[5] which predicts the diffusion probability in terms of the dislocation distance of the "nodal regions". In the case of prehistory we speak often about tribal groups (culture, settlements, technology etc.). It follows, that such question (diffusion of the innovation) could be interpreted as communication function between a huge number of individuals or as the relationship between intelligibility and hierarchy of a place if we prefer to adopt Lynch's terminology. The resistance relative to innovation absorption is calculated by the formula:

(3) $\quad p = P/1+e^{'a - \delta}$ [Berry].

[p represents the innovation adoption from population per cent; P the maximum percent of adopters; ^{a} value of p in time; $^\circ$ constant which fix p growth in time]

DISCUSSION: WHAT ABOUT GOALS?

The aim of space syntax analysis is to find an explanation for certain aspects of human behaviour and their relation to the environment that humans inhabit. In this manner we connect spacescape with movement, with local areas and their names (toponomastic). Naming the space could define a predictable pattern of movement and this would equal to the morphology of space. Indeed, predictability correlates space with movement and intelligibility links local and global boundaries.

Boundaries theory becomes useful by introducing an important structured element of syntax in the "reading" of prehistoric sites: the choice of place (Peponis *et alii*, 1990; Dimitriadis, 2003). Being able to choose is not only a philosophical question but also a question of "quality perception" of the spacescape. An integration process could be embedded into our movement on the landscape

---

[2] See also Dimitriadis, G. (2003). Il Linguaggio delle coppelle. Modello Tipologico basato sulla loro Struttura Geometrica. In Seglie, D. *et alii* (Eds.) 2007, 2' Congresso Internazionale "Ricerche Paletnologiche nelle Alpi Occidentali" & 3' Incontro "Arte Rupestre Alpina", Pinerolo (TO), 2003. The problem discussed in that paper was relative to the collocation of the cup-marked stones disseminated around the alpine area. I proposed an alternative model theory tending to explain how prehistoric man built up his "bound", how he moved along specific directions and how it is possible today to read this "cultural" traits.

[3] "Grid" models often are implemented by: 1. settlements distribution models; 2. density and population dimension systems of analysis.

[4] An alternative definition could be "space functionality".

[5] It's a bio-geophysical simulation models protocol.

which stimulates the visibility of action (Turner & Penn, 1999). By applying the SSA approach it may be possible to collect the essence of the prehistoric thought in order to recognise ideas attached to land and materials.

References

BAILEY, D.W. (1993) - Cronotypic tension in Bulgarian prehistory: 6500-3500 BC. *World Archaeology*. London. 25, p. 204-222.

BENEDIKT, M.L. (1979) - To take hold of space: isovists and isovist fields. *Environment and Planning B*. 6, p. 47-65.

BERRY, B. J.L. (1959) - Ribbon developments is the urban business pattern. *Annals of the Association of American Geographers*. 49, p.145-155.

BINFORD, L. (1981) - Behavioural archaeology and the Pompeii premise. *Journal of Anthropological Research*. 37, p. 195-208.

BINTLIFF, J. (ed.) (1991) - *The Annales School and Archaeology*. Leicester: Leicester University Press.

BLOCH, M. (1954) - *The Historian's Craft*. Manchester: Manchester University Press.

DALTON, R.C.; BANFA, S. (2003) - The syntactical image of the city: A reciprocal definition of spatial elements and spatial syntaxes", *Proceedings 4th International Space Syntax Symposium*, Vol. London.

DIMITRIADIS, G. (2003) - Il Linguaggio delle coppelle. Modello Tipologico basato sulla loro Struttura Geometrica. In SEGLIE, D. *et alii*, eds.- *II Congresso Internazionale "Ricerche Paletnologiche nelle Alpi Occidentali" & 3rd Incontro "Arte Rupestre Alpina"*. Pinerolo.

DIMITRIADIS, G. (2003) - Analytic Rock Art: a new Methodological Approach. *In VI Symposium Internacional de Arte Rupestre*. San Salvador de Jujuy: (forthcoming).

DIMITRIADIS, G. (2006) - Bronze age cosmology and rock art images. Solar ships, deer and charts. *Mediterranean Archaeology and Archaeometry, Special Issue*. 6, No .3, p. 143-148.

DIMITRIADIS, G. (2006a) - From Palaeolithic *Venus* up to the anthropomorphic *statue-menhir*. The ideological evolution of the human body in prehistoric art. In ZACHARACOPOULOU, E., ed. - *Beyond the Mind-Body Dualism: Psychoanalysis and the Human Body. Proceedings of the 6th Delphi International Psychoanalytic Symposium*. Delphi: ICS-Elsevier 1286, p. 7-12.

FRIEDMAN, J. (1982) - Catastrophe and continuity in social evolution. In RENFREW, C. ROWLANDS, M.; SEAGRAVE, B.A., eds. - *Theory and Explanation in Archaeology*. London: Academic Press.

GUREVICH, A. (1995) - The French historical evolution. The Annales School. In HODDER, I. *et alii*., eds.- *Interpreting Archaeology: Finding Meaning in the Past*. London: Routledge, p.158-161.

HÄGERSTRAND, T. (1970) - What about people in regional science? *Papers of the Regional Science Association*. 24, p. 7-21.

HARRIS, E.C. (1989) - *Principles of Archaeological Stratigraphy*. London: Academic Press.

HILLIER, B. (1999) - Space is the Machine: A Configura-tional Theory of Architecture. *Cambridge: Cambridge University Press*.

HILLIER, B.; HANSON, J. (1984). The Social Logic of Space. *Cambridge: Cambridge University Press*.

HILLIER, B.; LEAMAN, A. (1975) - The architecture of architecture. Foundations of a mathematical theory of artificial space. In HAWKES, D.,ed.- *Models and Systems in Architecture and Building*. Cambridge: The Construction Press.

HILLIER, B.; PENN, A. (2004). Rejoinder to Carlo Ratti. *Environment and Planning B - Planning and Design*. 31 (4), p. 487–499.

HILLIER, B. *et alii*. (1983) - Space Syntax, a different urban perspective. *Architects' Journal*. 30 Nov. 1983, p. 47-63.

HODDER, I. (ed.) (1987) - *Archaeology as Long-term History*. Cambridge: Cambridge University Press.

HOFSTADTER, R. D. (1979) - *Gödel, Escher, Bach: an Eternal Golden Braid*. Basik Books, INC.

KNAPP, C. (1992) - *Archaeology, Annales and Ethnohistory*. Cambridge: Cambridge Univesrity Press.

LUCAS, G. (2005) - *The Archaeology of Time*. London: Routledge.

LYNCH, K. (1960) - *The Image of the City*. Cambridge MA: MIT Press.

MCGLADE, J. (1987) - Chronos and the oracle: some thoughts on time, time scales and simulation. *Archaeological review from Cambridge*. Cambridge. 6, p. 21-31.

MCGLADE, J. (1999) - The times of history: archaeology, narrative and linear causality. In MILLER, T. (ed.) - *Time and Archaeology*. London: Routledge.

MIZOGUCHI, K. (1993) - Time in the reproduction of mortuary practices. *World Archaeology*. London. 25, p. 223-35.

MORRILL, R.L. (1974) - *The spatial organization of society*. Belmont: Duxbury Press, p.155.

NASH, R.F. (1982) - Wilderness and the American Mind. *New Haven: Yale University Press*.

PEPONIS, J. (1997) - Geometries of Architectural Description: shape and spatial configuration. In *Proceedings 1st International Space Syntax Symposium*, Vol. II. London.

PEPONIS, *et alii*. (1998) - On the generation of linear representations of spatial configurations. *Environment and Planning B*. 24, p. 761-781.

PRIGOGINE, I.; STENGERS, I. (1984) - *Order out of Chaos: Man's New Dialogue with Nature*. London: Fontana Paperbacks.

RATTI, C. (2004). Space syntax: some inconsistencies. *Environment and Planning B - Planning and Design*. 31(4), p. 501–511.

RENFREW, C.; COOK, K.L. (eds.) (1979) - *Trasformations. Mathematical Approaches to Culture Change*. London: Academic Press.

RICHARDSON, J.; KROEBER, A.L. (1952) - Three centuries of women's dress fashions: a quantitative analysis. In KROEBER, A.L., ed. - *The Nature of Culture*. Chicago: University of Chicago Press.

SCHIFFER, M.B. (1976) - *Behavioural Archaeology*. New York: Academic Press.

SOJA, E. (2001) - In Different Spaces. In *Proceedings 3rd International Space Syntax Symposium*, Atlanta.

THOM, R. (1972) - *Stabilité structurelle et morphogenèse*. Paris: InterÉditions.

THOMAS, J. (1996) - *Time, Culture and Identity. An Interpretative Archaeology*. London: Routledge.

TURNER, P.A.; PENN, A. (1999) - Making isovists syntactic: isovist integration analysis. In *Proceedings 2nd International Space Syntax Symposium*. Brasília: Universidade do Brasil, Vol. 1.08.

TVERSKY, B. (2001) - Structures of Mental space. In *Proceedings 3rd International Space Syntax Symposium*, Atlanta.

VAN DER LEEUW, S.; MCGLADE, J. (1997) - Introduction: archaeology and non-linear dynamics – new approaches to long-term change. In VAN DER LEEUW, S.; MCGLAD, J. eds., - *Time, Process and Structured Transformation in Archaeology*. London: Routledge.

NEOLITHIC CODES - A DIFFERENT APPROACH OF CUCUTENI WOMAN (PARA-ARCHEAEOLOGICAL AND PARA-MEDICAL MEDITATIVE ESSAY)

Romeo DUMITRESCU

Cucuteni pentru Mileniul III Foundation

Abstract: The essay brings an interdisciplinary approach to the interpretations of female statues discovered in the settlements from Isaiia - Balta Popii (jud. Iași) and Poduri – Dealul Ghindaru (jud. Bacău), both belonging to Pre-cucuteni culture. Proposing a very different and original explanation for the two assemblies of statues, the author uses general medical data. The main theory is that each assembly of statues represents a scheme of the female fertile period/cycle and the ideal menstrual period.
Keywords: female statues, signs, fertility, sexuality.

Résumé: Notre papier propose une approche interdisciplinaire sur l'interprétation des figurines féminines découvertes dans les sites de Isaiia – Balta Popii (dép. de Iași) et Poduri – Dealul Ghindaru (dép. de Bacău), dans des niveaux appartenant à la culture Precucuteni. Comme réponse aux problèmes que les deux complexes, qui contiennent chaque 21 représentations féminines, ont posées aux chercheurs, ont présente une théorie qui part des dates offertes par la médicine générale. Cette approche nous conduit vers l'hypothèse que chaque complexe représente un schéma de la période fertile et du periode menstruel idéal.
Mots clés : figurines féminines, gestes, fertilité, sexuel.

We have been questioning for centuries about the woman's role in the society and we could be writing tomes on the topic. In the modern world woman occupies different positions: secretary, model, worker, sportive, mother, etc. What was the woman in Cucuteni culture? Deity? Priestess? Clan ruler? Cook? Warrior? Mother?

First of all, one must wonder, why so many female representations in Cucuteni culture. If one is to draft a statistical report, one would find one male statue in fifty female representations. Based on this proportion, it is easy to fall into a trap. Today in the Orthodox and Catholic churches we find more representations of angels than that of Christ, the Virgin or even God. The most important are the least represented!

Over the centuries, the woman's role encountered major transformations in graphical representations in the pantheon, or in the decorative style of an epoch, and as percentage in different human activities, according to religious canon, tradition, society. Today it is highly unlikely to open a book, a newspaper, a magazine without finding female representations (images).

Were these statues only used as toys for children? Why in Cucuteni as well? The ratio of fifty female representations to one male should make us wonder! Why so many female statues? Why so many small chairs? Why are these artifacts being discovered both outside and inside the dwellings? Why most of them are broken, very rarely there have been discovered one intact? Why is the woman's body representation very schematic and, in contrast, so descriptive regarding the sexual features (the pubic triangle, the breasts, the hips, the bottom), while there is a total overlooking of the rest of the body?

As an unexpected present from Poduri-*Dealul Ghindaru*, Prof. Monah, and from Isaiia-*Balta Popii*, Prof. Ursulescu and Arch. Merlan, two settlements situated approximately 200 km away one from the other, two "boxes" with 21 female statues and 13 small chairs with different symbols were discovered (Fig. 7.1, 7.2). Similar discoveries were made at Sabatinovka and Ovcearovo, but the most noted and important are the ones mentioned above.

Other questions arise: why 21 female statues? Why 13 chairs? Why 21 cones and 42 small balls were also discovered at Isaiia? Why aren't the statues identical in shape, decoration and dimensions? Why some of them are represented with breasts, while others not? Why some chairs have symbols and others not and why they have different dimensions? Why are the sexual features most extensively described (breasts, pubic triangle, etc.)? Why only 7 statues have breasts? While at Poduri 10 have breasts? Why do three of them have their belly dotted with spots? Why do four of them have their legs apart and spots or incisions on their thighs and shanks?

Nevertheless, it is for the first time that female statues are gathered together with cones, small balls and chairs, in a box (Poduri and Isaiia discoveries). We can easily assume that the cones and the small balls stands for phallic representations. Still we are left with the small chairs and the statues.

I have pondered over my Gynaecology courses from university and read a lot on the issue, and I consequently dare to examine these archaeological discoveries with a doctor's eye. I would start with a brief lesson of physiology. Medical books say about the woman's period that it lasts between 21-35 days, during which time the mucous develops and retracts, and then is eliminated for

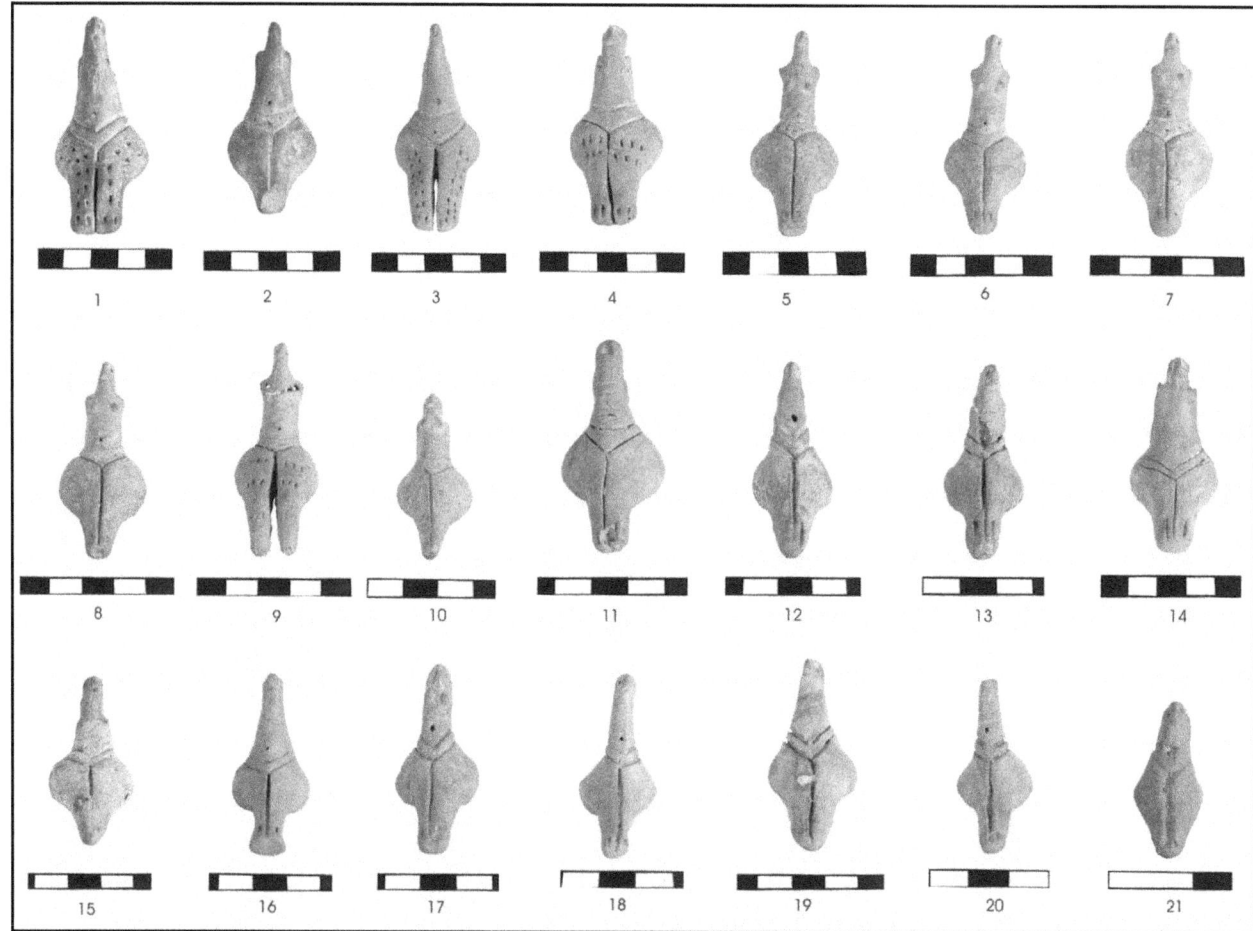

Fig. 7.1. The assemblie of statues from Isaiia - *Balta Popii* (county of Iassy).

three up to five days (all these unfold during 21 to 35 days).

This happens due to certain hormones: estrogen, progesterone and luthein hormone. Medical books also say that today the 21 days period is seldom met (especially in Guyana, Central Africa, and isolated populations from mountainous areas). This type of period is genetically inherited (a mother with 21 days period will have a daughter with 21 days period, and the ultra-fertile phase, between 13-15 days). This is a scheme of the 21 days period (Fig. 7.3).

For didactical reasons I have attributed each day a statue and a small chair. Arranged according to this period calendar, I am suggesting the following groups: 4 statues with legs apart, 9 simple statues with small chairs, 7 statues with breasts, 3 statues with belly incisions, 2 belonging to the 7 with breasts (Fig. 7.1).

I would try to order the statues with legs apart. First, these might describe menstruation (incisions or colour on thighs and shanks). Furthermore, at the statues from Poduri even the clothing decoration is different at the 4 or 5 statues. I would place on the next 9 chairs the statues without breasts, and finally, the statues with breasts. Statue no. XIII has an incision on the belly and the chair on which she is sitting has, on the upper side, a sign of the pubic triangle. The next 7 statues have breasts and the first have belly incisions. The last statue is extremely small, very much like an embryonic structure.

If I were to overlap the scientific schemes of a monthly period, we mind find a somewhat "logical" explanation. Thus, the final arrangement would be the following: the first 4 with legs apart would correspond to the menstrual period. Here we have a chair which is different from all others: the upper side of the chair is a dotted spiral, while the lower side is a XIX design, which is to be found on the upper side of another chair, discovered by chance at Poduri, which might signify a sexual interdiction.

In the Bible we have an absolute interdiction to have sex during this period, followed by a period of non-cleanliness, which could correspond with the next statues.

My medical opinions is that, in a period when might resided in number, Pre-cucuteni and Cucuteni people needed more children. This assembly of statues represents a scheme of the fertile female cycle/period. Probably, each young couple received as a gift this "fertility-kit" upon getting married. By comparing the menstrual cycle

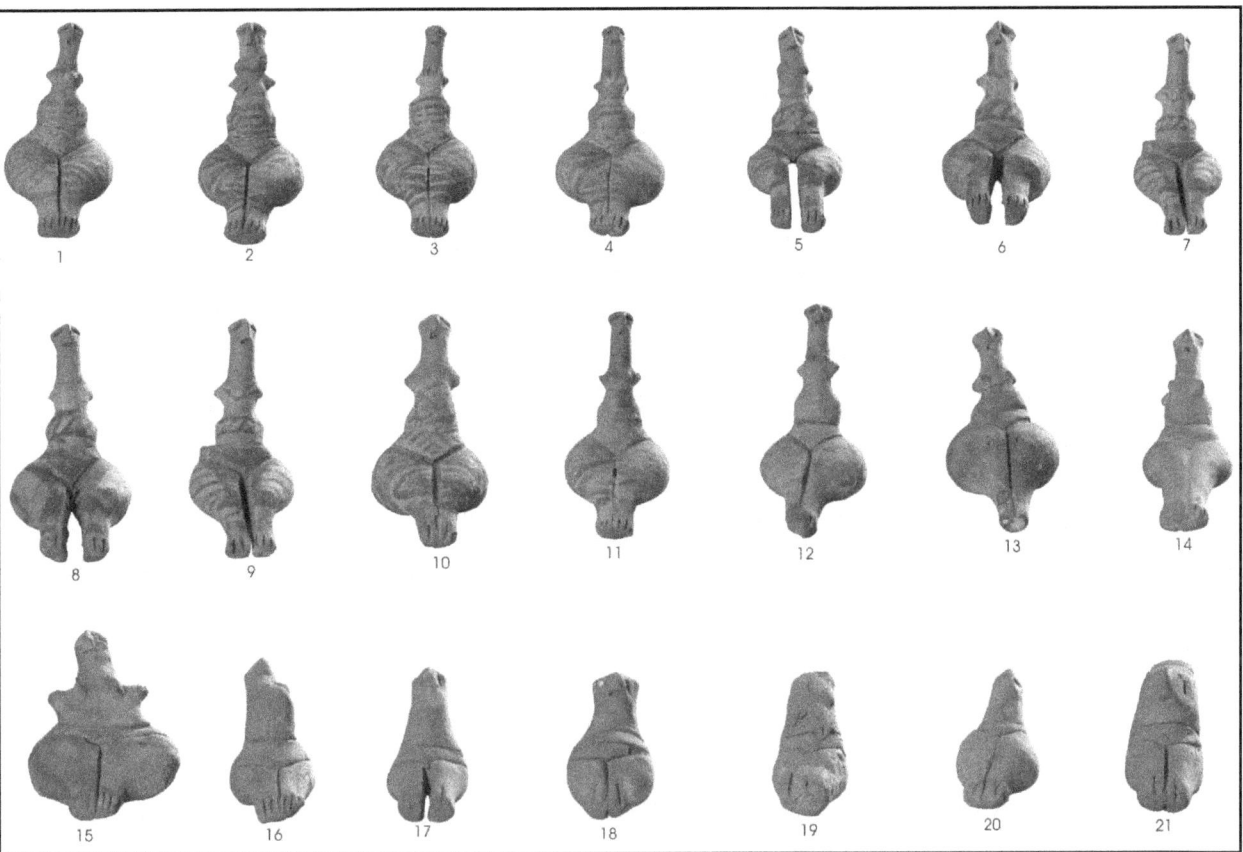

Fig. 7.2. The assemblie of statues from Poduri - *Dealul Ghindaru* (county of Bacau).

predominant today, of 28 days, with the Cucuteni one, of 21 days, it is likely that their fertility range was 30% bigger than ours, (until the emergence of modern contraceptives). This might explain the demographic explosion in Pre-cucuteni and Cucuteni time. Probably, upon the menopause or woman's death, these kits were thrown away, and the statues broken in a ritual fashion. My opinion is based on the presence of the cones, phalluses corresponding to the 21 statues, and on the signs on the chairs, as well on the focus on female genitals and therefore I conclude that these kits were a metaphor for sexuality and conception. Even they would refer to a normal menstrual cycle of 28 days, the statues could be re-arranged to maintain the theory valid. In Isaiia set we have smaller earth-ware spheres perforated to which we don't have, yet, a reasonable explanation. They could represent the days for completing the menstrual cycle of 28 days.

3000 years from now, our houses would be researched by an archaeologist, and is likely that he will find an album with photos of or beloved wife or girlfriend, a pack of 21 contraceptive pills, a condom box and a pregnancy test and he will wonder why there so many female images in the photo album, why there are 21 small spheres; he will wonder on the use of the other objects and why our civilization has perished. He will ask himself if these are cult objects, idols, matriarchy symbols, and why 21 small pink spheres. All we can do is to sit and ponder over the world, as they did, and just as the Târpești thinker did 6000 years ago.

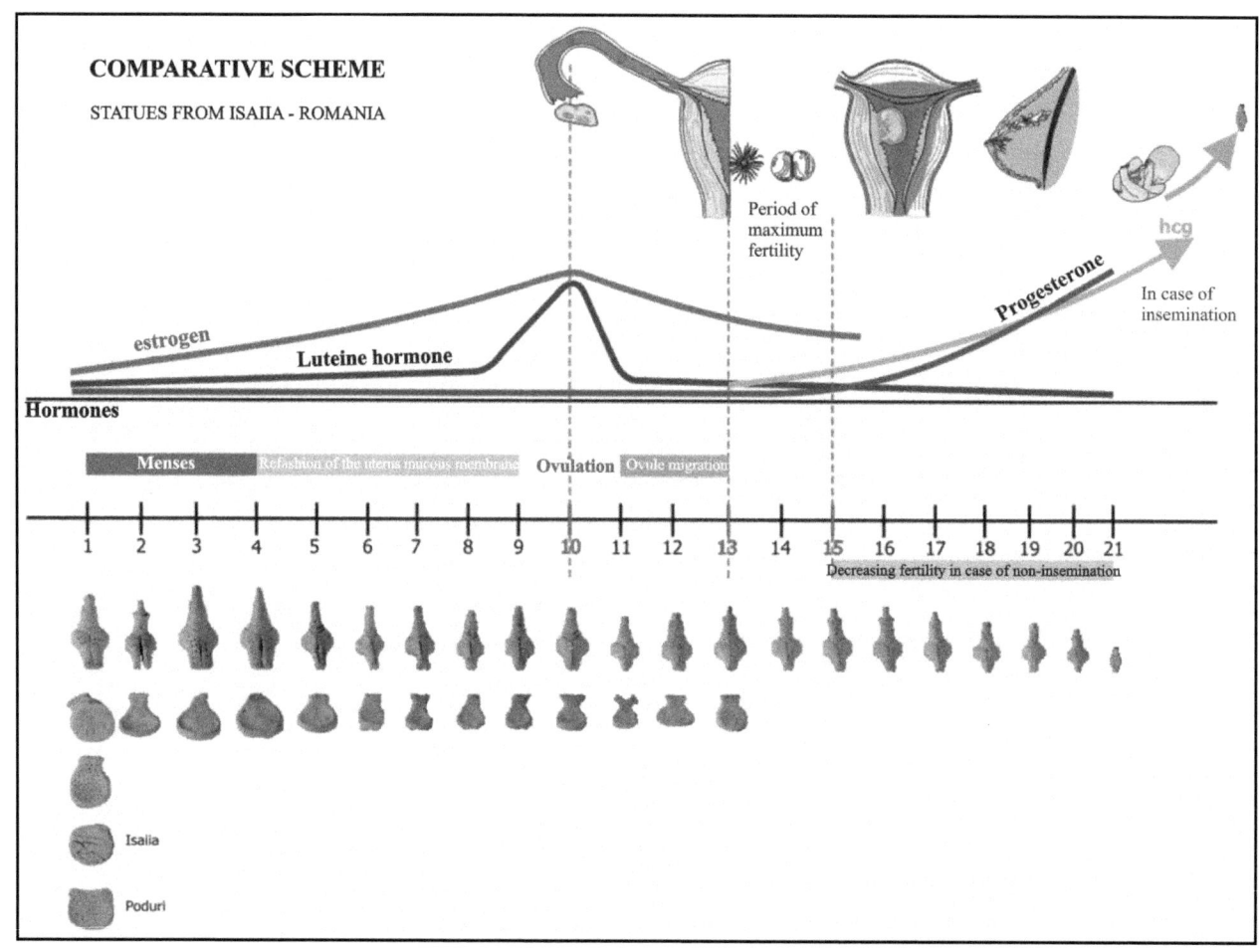

Fig. 7.3. Comparative representation of 21 days period and the 21 statues from the site of Isaiia - *Balta Popii*.

SIMBOLISM WITHIN TECHNOLOGY

Dragos GHEORGHIU
Department of Research, National University of Arts (Bucharest)

Abstract: *The author believes that an area where Cognitive Archaeology could be perceived as Symbolic Archaeology is the study of technologies.*
In current research it seems customarily to separate the study of technologies/ chaînes-opératoires from the study of symbolism, since we overlook the fact that technologies, like all the pre-Modern cultural aspects, could be activities with a high symbolic content beside their functional character.
The present paper will analyse some of the formative technologies of building in the East European Chalcolithic clay cultures, focussing on the symbolism of cyclical processes of construction and deconstruction of objects identified in the material culture of the studied area, and exemplified with two study-cases (the building/deconstruction of houses and of anthropomorphic figurines).
Key-words : Cognitive Archaeology, chaînes-opératoires, East European Chalcolithic, construction and deconstruction

Résumé : *Selon l'avis de l'auteur, le domaine ou l'archéologie cognitive peut être percue comme une archéologie symbolique est celui des technologies.*
Dans la recherche contemporaine la séparation entre l'étude des technologies/ des chaînes-opératoires/ et l'étude du symbolisme semble normale, a cause de l'ignorance du fait que toutes les activitées pré-Modernes pouvait avoir un caractère symbolique, à coté de leur caractère fonctionnel.
L'article analyse les technologies de construction dans les cultures Chalcolithiques de L'Éurope de l'Est, en se concentrant sur le symbolisme des processus cycliques de construction et de déconstruction des objets, spécifique pour la culture materielle de l'époque, et exemplifiés dans deux cas (la construction/déconstruction des maisons et des figurines céramiques anthropomorphes).
Mots clés: Archéologie cognitive, chaînes-opératoires, Chalcolithique de L'Éurope de l'Est, construction et déconstruction

The tendency from the anthropological research to separate the symbolic representations from cognition, i.e. to separate "culture as public ideology" from "culture as knowledge" (Keller and Keller, 1996: 172; see also Norman, 1993), seems not to operate so strict since processualist archaeologists recognized the symbolic approach as a mode of thought (see Renfrew and Zubrow 1997).

As Justeson and Stephens (1997: 167) pointed out, "[c]ognition refers to the representation of knowledge and to the process of operating on those representations; a 'cognitive archaeology' would investigate aspects of knowledge representation and information processing which are recoverable from the archaeological record". In such a perspective symbolic though is integrated to the cognitive field, because it covers all human activities (see Cassirer, 1945), to cite only some of them, accepted by archaeologists: design, planning, measurement, social relations, the supernatural, and [the] representation[s] (Renfrew, 1997: 6).

For two decades a "cognitive war" (Zubrow, 1997: 108) separated two schools of thought, the humanistic one, based on hermeneutics and symbolism, and the processual one, based on positivism, but which in a final phase, approached the study of palaeo-cognition, which included symbolism.

There is general agreement that symbolism is to be finding in objects, assemblages and rituals and never *within* technologies, therefore the aim of the paper would be to discover symbolic values hidden within the technological process (Gheorghiu, 2005a).

THE CONCEPT OF CHAÎNE OPÉRATOIRE

It is only recently that the pioneering studies on technology of the French school (see Leroi-Gourhan, 1964 ; Leroi-Gourhan, 1965; Lemonnier, 1983), unjustly neglected for decades were adopted by British-American archaeologists (see Dobres, 2000), who now recognize the importance of the *chaîne opératoire*.

A *chaîne opératoire* is a process consisting of a "series of operations which transforms a substance from a raw material into a manufactured product" (Van der Leeuw, 2002: 240). A *chaîne opératoire* is formed of two types of stages: "objective", "correspond[ing] to operations (…) which can be neither altered, eliminated, or replaced without seriously affecting the result" (Lemonnier, 1986: 155), because of the constraints of the materials, and labelled by Lemonnier (1983: 17) "strategical" or by Schlanger (1997 : 144) "fixed", and "subjective", labelled by Van der Leeuw (1997 : 136) as "flexible", when the operator can choose between alternative actions (see Lemonnier, 1986: 155; Van der Leeuw, 2002: 240).

As the result of a symbiosis between a technical action and a symbolic decision, a *chaîne opératoire* is a processual – cognitive and symbolic action, situated between the know-how of the technical production, and a cultural implication on which the technical production depends (see Karlin and Julien, 1997: 154) more or less. On one hand, there is the immutable determinism of the material and on the other hand, there are the symbolic decisions issued from the dominant symbols of the epoch. From the study of Lower Danube Neolitic and Chalcolithic material culture, I believe that in prehistoric societies the subjective stages are in fact determined by the cultural decision of the community and are the locations where symbolic information is inserted.

STUDY CASES

In order to present this symbiosis, I will begin with an example of symbolic decision within the *chaîne opératoire* which is the "choice of the potter", identified in ethnoarhaeological study cases (see Van der Leeuw, 1997; Gosselain, 2002) and inferred in ethnoarchaeology. One of the most explicit moments of a subjective decision is the selection of the temper of the paste, which in not determined by the other stages of the making of the clay objects.

In the Neolithic Starčevo tradition (see Manson, 1995) one can observe in time a tendency to use as temper the very fine cut chaff from the cattle's dung for the coarse and semi-coarse pottery. Seen from the perspective of the technical decision the use of the dung as temper could have had practical reasons, since it augment the plasticity of the clay paste, produces an even drying and a good firing, and intensify the thermal conductivity of the ceramic containers. However, such choice could have been a symbolic decision, and would insist on the economic option of cattle breeding of the Starčevo communities.

Another example is the technique of construction-deconstruction of Chalcolithic material culture, exemplified with the anthropomorphic figurines from the Cucuteni-Tripolye tradition, because the very fragmentary state of these ceramic figurines infers the possibility of the existence of a symbolic process of controlled deconstructtion, included within their very technology of making (see Gheorghiu, 2005b).

Through experiments, one can see that the inception of the modelling of the body shape starts always from a technical but also a symbolic decision, i.e. the formation of three clay balls of the same dimension, one forming the torso and the two other the feet of the figurine (Gheorghiu, 2005b).

An important stage of the *chaîne opératoire* of the figurine making was the fastening of the feet together; this operation being achieved during the first two phases of the tradition (A and A-B) by means of a twist of the point of the feet between the thumb and the forefinger. Such operation allowed an easy deconstruction when the point of the feet was broken.

In the final phase of the tradition (B) the *chaîne opératoire* is the same except for the mode of fastening the feet, performed through the rubbing of the two modules between the palms, this method forming an extra cone prolonging the feet of the figurines. I believe this conical protuberance would have had the role of a better thrusting the figurine into a soft substance, probably foodstuff (Gheorghiu, 2001) which made the figurines more visible during their ritual use.

DISCUSSION

From the examples presented, one can see that the symbolic stages within the *chaîne opératoire* could have had a technical motivation too, but that they can change in time without transforming the structure of the technological action.

In my opinion the syntagm "choice of the individual" mentioned during the present text does not represent a reality of the prehistoric societies, since any cultural decision was taken by the community in accordance with its dominant symbols, as the uniformity of the *chaîne opératoire* demonstrates.

The two study cases support the idea that the subjective stages could contain information about the dominant symbols which could be incorporated within the technology of making of the objects in a less or more visible way.

Therefore in the Starčevo tradition the use of the dung as temper could have been a message related to the dominant economy and symbolism, and the passage in time from the organic temper to inorganic could be interpreted not only as an improvement of the relationship with fire of the ceramic containers but also as a symbolic message hidden within the technology of making of ceramic objects about the transition from the cattle breeding economy to one based on the domestication and conquest of the land.

The example from Cucuteni-Tripolye demonstrates that a new ritual can be visualized with a modification of a subjective stage of the *chaîne opératoire* of construction of the figurines.

I conclude that a *chaîne opératoire* is a cognitive message more complex as perceived until today, and the study of the symbolism within it will add new data to the study of ancient cognition.

References

CASSIRER, E. (1945) - *An essay on man*. New Haven: Yale University Press, 237 p.

DOBRES, M.-A. (2000) - *Technology and social agency. Outlining a practice framework for archaeology*, Oxford, Malden: Balckwell, 300 p.

GHEORGHIU, D. (2001) - The cult of ancestors in East European Chalcolithic: A holographic approach. In BIEHL, P.; BERTHEMES, F., eds, - *The Archaeology of Cult*. Budapest: Archaeolingua, pp. 73-88.

GHEORGHIU, D. (2005a) - *Symbolic technologies*, www.semioticon.com

GHEORGHIU, D. (2005b) - The Controlled fragmentation of anthropomorphic figurines, *Cucuteni*, Piatra Neamt. In DUMITROAIA, G.; CHAPMAN, J., WELLER, O.; PREOTEASA, C.; MUNTEANU, R.; NICOLA, D.; MONAH, D., eds. - *Cucuteni. 120 years of research. Time to sum up*. Piatra-Neamt, Constantin Matasa, p. 137-144.

GOSSELAIN, O. P. (2002) - *Poteries du Cameroun méridional. Styles techniques et rapports à l'identité*, Paris: CNRS Editions, 254 p.

JUSTESON, J.S.; STEPHENS, L.D. (1997) - Variation and change in symbol systems: case studies in Elamite cuneiform. In RENFREW, C.; ZUBROW, E. eds - *The ancient mind. Elements of cognitive archaeology*. Cambridge: Cambridge University Press, p. 167-175.

KARLIN, C.; JULIEN, M. (1997) - Prehistoric technology: a cognitive science? In RENFREW, C.; ZUBROW, E. eds - *The Ancient mind. Elements of cognitive Archaeology*. Cambridge: Cambridge University Press, p. 152-164.

KELLER, C.M.; KELLER, J.D. (1996) - *Cognition and tool use. The blacksmith at work*. Cambridge: Cambridge University Press, 200 p.

LEMONNIER, P. (1983) - L'Etude des systèmes téchniques, une urgence en technologie culturelle. *Techniques et culture* 1, Edition de la Maison des Sciences de l'Homme Paris, p. 12-27.

LEMONNIER, P. (1986) - The Study of Material Culture Today. Toward an Anthropology of Technical Systems. *Journal of Anthropological Archaeology*. 5, Amsterdam, pp. 147-184.

LEROI-GOURHAN, A. (1964) - *Le Geste et la Parole I – technique et language*. Paris : Albin Michel. 323 p.

LEROI-GOURHAN, A. (1965) - *Le Geste et la Parole II – la mémoire et le rythmes*. Paris: Albin Michel, 285 p.

MANSON, J. I. (1995) - Starčevo pottery and Neolithic development in the Central Balkans. In BARNETT, W.; HOOPES, J. W., eds. - *The Emergence of Pottery. Technology and innovation in ancient societies*. Washington and London: Smithsonian Institution Press, pp. 65-77.

NORMAN, D. (1993) - Cognition in the head and in the world: An introduction, In GREENO, J. G. ed. - *Situated action*, Special Issue of *Cognitive Science*, 17 (1), pp. 1-6.

RENFREW, C. (1997) - Towards a cognitive archaeology. In RENFREW, C.; ZUBROW, E. eds - *The ancient mind. Elements of cognitive archaeology*: Cambridge: Cambridge University Press, pp. 3-12.

RENFREW, C.; ZUBROW, E., (1997) - *The ancient mind. Elements of cognitive Archaeology*. Cambridge: Cambridge University Press, p. 195.

SCHLANGER, N. (1997) - Mindful technology: unleashing the *chaine operatoire* for an archaeology of mind. In RENFREW, C.; ZUBROW, E. eds - *The Ancient mind. Elements of cognitive archaeology*. Cambridge: Cambridge University Press, pp.143-151.

VAN DER LEEUW, S.E. (1997) - Cognitive aspects of "technique". In RENFREW, C.; ZUBROW, E. eds - *The Ancient mind. Elements of cognitive archaeology*. Cambridge: Cambridge University Press, pp. 135-142.

VAN DER LEEUW, S.E. (2002) - Giving the potter a choice. In LEMONNIER, P. ed. - *Technical choices. Transformations in material cultures since the Neolithic*. London, New York: Routledge, pp. 238-288.

ZUBROW, E. (1997) - Knowledge representation and archaeology: a cognitive example using GIS. In RENFREW, C.; ZUBROW, E. eds - *The ancient mind. Elements of cognitive archaeology*. Cambridge: Cambridge University Press, p.107-118.

ORGANISATION D'UN SANCTUAIRE RUPESTRE : LES ROCHERS DE CREYSSEILLES (ARDECHE, FRANCE)

Philippe HAMEAU

Laboratoire d'Anthropologie "Identité, Mémoire et Cognition sociale" (LAMIC),
Université de Nice-Sophia Antipolis (hameau@unice.fr)

Résumé : Les 68 rochers gravés du plateau de Creysseilles sont répartis en deux concentrations séparées par un petit talweg. Dans chacun des groupes, le choix des rochers n'est pas fortuit. Certains ont été apportés d'une carrière proche. L'iconographie est différente dans chacun des groupes: cupule et signe anthropomorphe masculin à l'ouest, cupule, signe anthropomorphe masculin et arceau à l'est. Cette distinction est analysée. La gravure de deux signes corniformes et de fines incisions sur des blocs de roche volcanique permettent d'évoquer les réutilisations des lieux après le Néolithique et jusqu'à l'époque moderne.
Mots-clés: art schématique, gravures rupestres, cupules, Néolithique, Creysseilles

Abstract: The sixty-eight engraved rocks of the Creysseilles' plateau are distributed on two concentrations separated by a little depression. In each group, there is a deliberate choice of certain rock surfaces. Some blocks were transported from a near quarry. Iconography is not identical in boths groups: association of the cupmark and the anthropomorphous male sign in the west area, association of the cupmark, the anthropomorphous male sign and the archlike sign in the west area. We analyse this distribution. Two horn-shaped engravings and thin incisions on volcanic blocks allows us to show the site has been in use after the Neolithic to the modern period.
Key-words: schematic art, engravings, cupmark, Neolithic, Creysseilles

PRESENTATION

Le groupe des rochers gravés de Creysseilles[1] occupe le rebord d'un plateau dominant la rive gauche du Mézayon, affluent de l'Ouvèze, à 760m d'altitude (Fig. 9.1a). La végétation dense de la pente fait place à une prairie colonisant la bande des grès triasiques qui traverse le département de l'Ardèche selon un axe NE-SO. Immédiatement au nord et à l'ouest émergent les basaltes des Coirons. Les parcelles étudiées sont essentiellement vouées au pacage des ovins et entrecoupées de pierriers.

Un des rochers gravés du site est signalé dès 1959 (Bellin 1959). Plus tard, ce rocher est appelé rocher des "Pieds du Diable" sur la foi de témoignages oraux. Neuf autres rochers gravés aux environs du premier sont alors publiés (Bellin *et al.* 1978). L'un d'eux porterait selon les auteurs la gravure d'un oiseau. L'ampleur du phénomène gravé, 68 rochers en tout, est révélée en 1990 lorsque D. Vaillant prospecte l'ensemble du plateau. En fait, deux sous groupes sont attestés: un groupe occidental de 50 rochers, dit des "Croix de Saint-André", du nom du quartier qui les porte et un groupe oriental de 18 rochers localisés autour des "Pieds du Diable". Les signes exprimés dans chaque zone, la configuration et l'organisation des lieux, l'importance du phénomène gravé, sont différents dans chaque zone. Nous nous efforcerons de montrer l'unité de ce groupe de rochers, sa mise en place progressive et les phénomènes de survivance qui s'y rattachent. Un petit promontoire proche du groupe oriental a restitué, en outre, des éléments lithiques qui nous permettent d'évoquer des activités en relation avec la présence des gravures.

LES DEUX ZONES GRAVEES

La zone occidentale

Les rochers sont disséminés sur la partie NO de la parcelle, celle qui est véritablement en rebord du plateau. La zone rupestre est donc naturellement délimitée sur trois côtés par un terrain en pente et couvre une surface de 210m (O-E) sur 160m (N-S). Une carrière encombrée de blocs occupe l'angle N-O de la zone.

Les rochers gravés sont tous sur le plateau, donc sur le replat et non sur la pente qui pourtant compte de nombreux supports propices à la gravure. On constate plusieurs concentrations de rochers, cinq en termes de proximité étroite, trois si l'on accepte des groupements plus lâches. Ces différentes concentrations sont approximativement parallèles et perpendiculaires à la pente. En fait, la géologie conditionne plus ou moins ces regroupements de rochers : une partie d'entre eux correspond à l'orientation des strates du substrat. Toutefois, certains blocs sont aussi plus éloignés des autres.

Le grès utilisé pour la gravure est généralement une roche à grain fin. Les graveurs ont négligé les supports trop fissurés ou les blocs dont la face supérieure est trop accidentée. On remarque un travail d'aplanissement pour quelques dalles solidaires du substrat. Cependant, ces observations ne représentent pas une règle absolue.

Dix-sept rochers, tous localisés dans la partie nord de la parcelle, ne sont pas solidaires du substrat. Il pouvait

---

[1] Cette intervention a été menée dans le cadre du programme de recherches P30 avec le soutien du Ministère de la Culture et l'aide de la commune de Saint-Julien-en-Saint-Alban, et des associations S.A.V.O. I.R. et A.S.E.R. du Centre-Var. Ont participé à cette intervention, 'A. Acovitsioti-Hameau, R. Rouziès, S. Rousseau, C. Chopin, C. Beaufeist, M. Delefosse, A. Magne, D., M.-C.et N. Vaillant et nous-même.

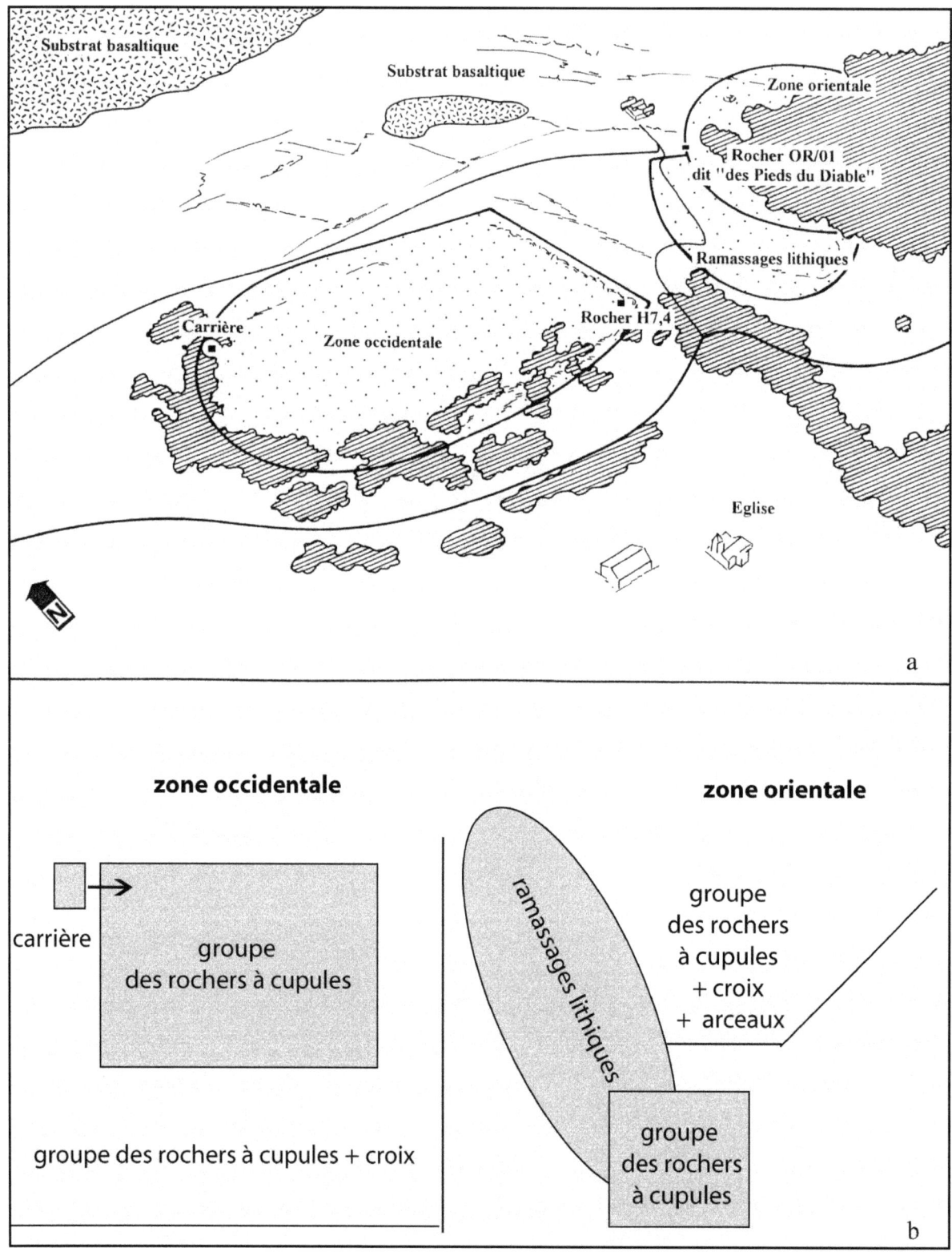

Fig. 9.1. a. Vue générale du site à partir d'une photographie aérienne : division des différents espaces ;
b. Organisation sémantique du sanctuaire.

s'agir de blocs trouvés *in situ* mais il semble que la plupart d'entre ont été extraits de la petite carrière déjà citée. Le front de taille lui-même, en L, avec une série d'entailles de forme conique du côté nord, porte des gravures. La dépression ainsi formée a été fouillée dans sa partie orientale. Le sédiment y est sableux, issu de la désagrégation du substrat et on y note plusieurs lits de blocs bruts de dimensions diverses. Aucun outil, lithique ou métallique, n'y a été retrouvé. Le volume de blocs gréseux extraits de la carrière est estimé à 15m³, volume largement supérieur à celui de l'ensemble des blocs non solidaires du substrat. Ces derniers sont généralement de petite taille: moyenne de 1,05mL x 0,65ml x 0,35mh, soit une masse de 550kg. Ils ont été transportés sur des distances allant de 35m à 210m. Ils l'ont été dans une zone où les affleurements de grès sont rares, voire inexistants. Il semble que les Préhistoriques aient apporté des blocs à graver là où ceux-ci manquaient. Ils les ont mis en forme (traces de découpe, échancrures) et mis en exergue en les surhaussant au moyen de petites dalles. Ces rochers que nous supposons déplacés portent presque tous des cupules à l'exception d'autres figures.

Les outils qui auraient pu servir au dégagement des blocs ou à l'exécution des gravures ne nous sont pas parvenus hormis deux fragments de galets de rivière sans traces d'usage apparent. L'extraction des blocs dans la carrière a pu être pratiquée à l'aide de coins de bois imbibés d'eau. Les cupules et les figures qui leur sont associées sont réalisées par piquetage du grès suivi d'un polissage par percussion posée tournée. Les traits allongés sont égalisés par un mouvement de va-et-vient.

Les gravures de cette zone expriment un corpus réduit où dominent les cupules. On compte 44 rochers portant au moins une cupule, 24 rochers ne portant que des cupules dont 7 sont monocupulaires. Les croix sont plus rares : 15 rochers portant au moins une croix dont 2 où ces croix sont les seules figures exécutées. L'association croix + cupule(s) existe dans 10 cas.

Les traits, simples ou en plusieurs exemplaires, accompagnent systématiquement les deux premières figures. L'association cupule(s) + trait(s) existe dans 8 cas et l'association croix + trait(s) dans 6 cas. Les autres figures, hache, main, sont en nombre si restreint qu'elles n'ont pas d'incidence sur la localisation des associations de signes.

On observe surtout une organisation des rochers différemment gravés. Les blocs portant des croix ont tendance à être périphériques au groupe et donc à encercler ceux qui ne sont gravés que de cupules. Or, cette constatation va de pair avec les concentrations de rochers signalées précédemment. En effet, dans chaque concentration existe la complémentarité cupule(s) + croix + trait(s). Ce fait explique sans doute la présence de quelques rochers avec croix et traits au milieu de la parcelle. Enfin, le rocher qui porte la décoration la plus abondante (198 cupules, 1 bassin, 2 rigoles, 3 croix, 1 main, nombreux traits) (Fig. 9.2a) est aussi le seul qui occupe une position réellement éminente, en débord sur la pente.

La zone orientale

Les rochers y sont strictement ordonnés en rebord de plateau et forment un long chapelet qui s'étire sur une distance de 500m environ. Seul le rocher des fameux "Pieds du Diable", s'écarte de cet alignement (Fig. 9.2c). Là encore, les rochers utilisés sont des grès à grain fin, peu fissurés et dont la face supérieure est lisse. Aucun travail de découpe ou de déplacement d'un bloc n'est observable excepté pour le rocher 07 (Fig. 9.2b), en débord sur la pente et soutenu par un autre bloc détaché du substrat. Un seul rocher montre des traces de mise en forme sur sa face verticale.

On n'observe aucun regroupement de rochers dans cette zone. En revanche, la décoration divise ce groupe oriental où les 6 premiers rochers, éloignés les uns des autres, sont peu gravés tandis que les 12 autres, moins distants, présentent une décoration diversifiée et exubérante.

Les gravures de cette zone expriment également un corpus réduit où dominent les cupules : 14 rochers portant au moins une cupule ou un bassin et 4 rochers ne portant que des cupules. Dans 10 cas, les cupules accompagnent une ou plusieurs croix et aucune croix n'est seule sur un rocher. La figure en arceau est présente sur 7 rochers de cette zone. Elle est toujours associée à la cupule et/ou à la croix. On compte 5 cas d'associations complètes arceau + croix + cupule(s) concernant les rochers les plus à l'est du groupe oriental.

Entre les deux zones gravées

Le site n'a pas fait l'objet de sondages excepté au niveau de la carrière et de quelques rochers déplacés dans la zone occidentale. En revanche, des prospections extensives ont été menées à plusieurs reprises. Une soixantaine de témoins lithiques ont été retrouvés entre les deux zones gravées, dans un vallon peu profond et très évasé, et sur un replat de 200m de côté.

Un fragment de lame épaisse appartient à un couteau, pièce à placer entre Néolithique moyen et final. La présence d'un nucléus, d'éclats corticaux de préparation, de petits éclats résultant ordinairement de la taille et d'éclats débités selon un principe identique à l'organisation du nucléus, prouve qu'une partie du mobilier lithique recueilli a été débitée sur place au détriment d'un silex jaunâtre. Un autre nucléus, de petite taille (L=1,6cm), à enlèvements lamellaires, laisse également présager une taille sur place. En revanche, des lamelles ont peut-être été apportées. La diversité des techniques de débitage, percussion et pression, celle des matières siliceuses, la facture de certains éléments, font penser à leur apport depuis quelque habitat situé aux environs du sanctuaire. Plusieurs éclats et lamelles sont retouchés et il semble que deux des lamelles portent un micropoli attribuable au travail des végétaux. Enfin, plusieurs pièces ont connu l'action du feu après leur débitage et façonnage. Nous ne saurions dater ce contact thermique.

La sobriété de ce mobilier lithique et la localisation des vestiges amoindrissent les possibilités d'une attribution chrono-culturelle des gravures elles-mêmes. Les gravures montrent de réelles analogies stylistiques avec les corpus,

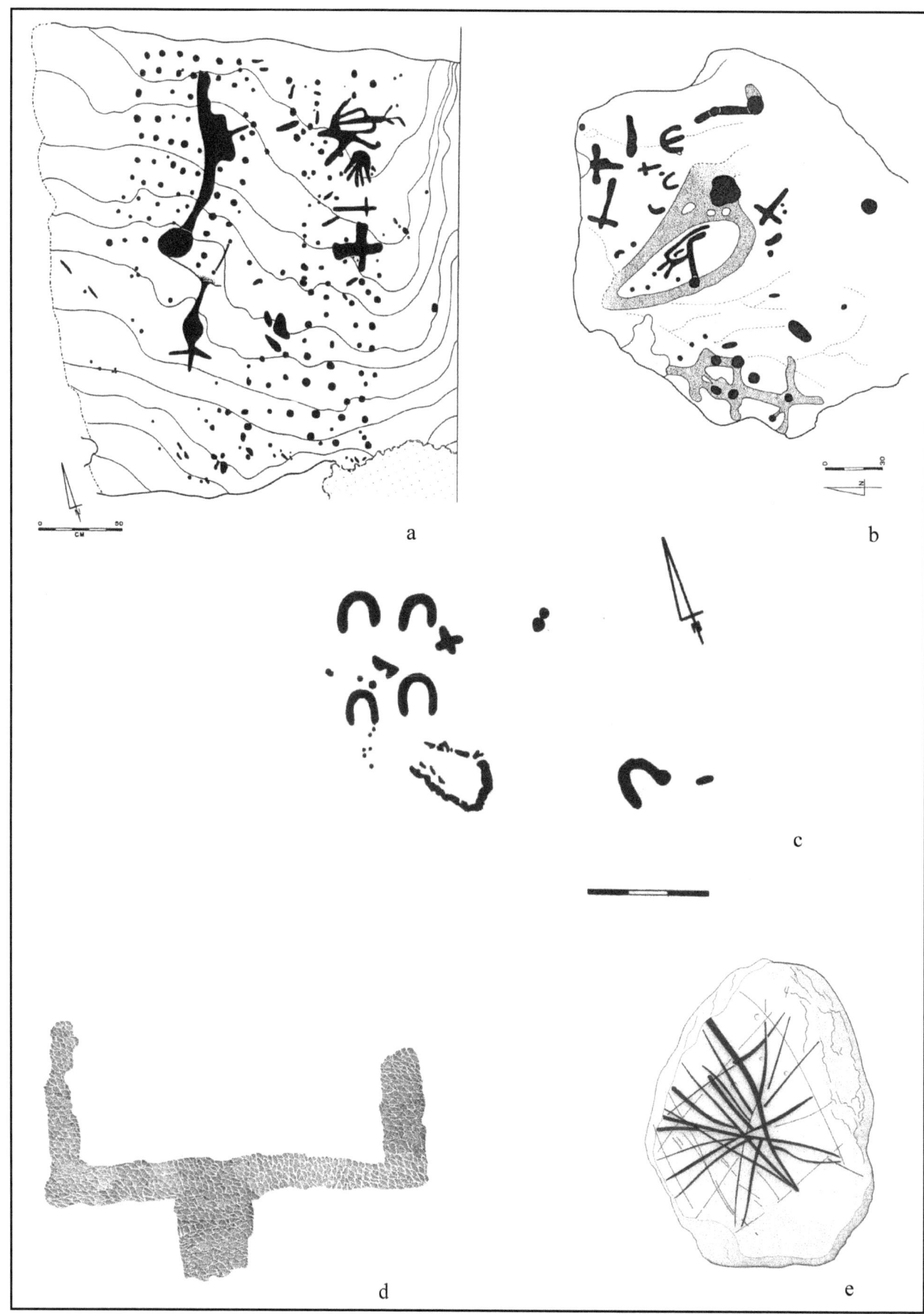

Fig. 9.2. a. le rocher H7.4 : zone occidentale ; b. le rocher OR.07 : zone orientale ; c. le rocher OR.01, dit des Pieds du Diable : zone orientale ; d. l'un des corniformes du rocher H7.4 ; e. un moellon de basalte avec gravures linéaires.

peint et sculpté, du sud de la France, que nous estimons aujourd'hui essentiellement attribuables au Néolithique moyen/final. Ce mobilier lithique très sommaire, serait sans doute à rapprocher d'autres cortèges plus conséquents pour lesquels nous avons émis l'hypothèse d'un débitage réalisé dans le cadre d'un apprentissage à la taille des matières siliceuses (Hameau 2002).

IMPLANTATION ET ORGANISATION DU SANCTUAIRE

Les supports

Le site de Creysseilles est un site de hauteur, dominant un vaste paysage. La vue est dégagée du côté sud, direction à prendre au sens large. Les lieux répondent donc aux deux paramètres que nous avons maintes fois évoqués à propos des sites ornés: le panoptisme et l'héliotropisme (Hameau, 1999).

Pour profiter d'un substrat relativement aisé à modeler, ce sanctuaire hypètre est implanté au niveau des grès qui affleurent sur une partie du département. Une telle concentration de roches gravées, sur une aussi faible superficie, reste exceptionnelle. L'accumulation observée à Creysseilles donne le sentiment d'un sanctuaire intensément fréquenté ou du moins d'un sanctuaire important. L'implantation mais aussi l'aménagement du site pourraient donc avoir été particulièrement réfléchis.

La zone choisie pour la gravure est l' extrême rebord du plateau. On constate un choix des rochers puisque tous ne sont pas utilisés. On peut penser que ce choix s'est porté sur des supports de bonne qualité. Des traces de mise en forme montrent que l'on a pallié certaines aspérités du support. Un piquetage léger de la surface supérieure des blocs a parfois aplani celle-ci. Des rochers sans doute trop anguleux ont été martelés sur leurs faces latérales. Mais, au-delà de la mise en valeur de certains rochers, l'emplacement de ceux-ci nous intéresse. On observe que 17 d'entre eux ont été apportés en des points précis de la zone occidentale. Ils ont été soigneusement calés de façon à présenter une face supérieure parfaitement horizontale. L'existence d'une carrière d'extraction de ces mêmes rochers est un fait exceptionnel. Elle suggère un travail collectif et des moyens mis en oeuvre très semblables à ceux qu'exigeait la construction d'un dolmen ou l'érection d'un menhir.

Bien que l'on constate l'existence de plusieurs concentrations de rochers dans la zone occidentale celles-ci n'ont apparemment aucun lien avec les rochers censément transportés. Ces blocs ont été indifféremment rajoutés à chacun des trois sous-groupes évoqués. Cet apport de blocs a été plus important dans les concentrations, occidentale et centrale, sans doute par manque de blocs affleurant dans la partie haute de la parcelle. L'agencement des blocs dans la zone orientale est moins net.

Enfin, nous avons signalé que deux rochers, un dans chaque zone, avaient été choisis ou déplacés en fonction de leur débord sur la pente : deux blocs en position particulièrement éminente sur le rebord du plateau.

Les signes

Les cupules sont en grand nombre et de diverses dimensions, de 2cm à 20cm de diamètre. Il n'est pas impossible que des cupules naturelles aient été utilisées et mises en forme.

La plupart de ces cupules sont disposées sans ordre apparent. Cependant, sur le rocher H7,4 nous observons plusieurs alignements parallèles. Sur d'autres rochers, une grande cupule est systématiquement flanquée d'une cupulette. Sur le rocher OR.17, l'alignement des cupules décrit un arc de cercle qui correspond à la bordure de la pierre et suit une progression métrique de l'ouest vers l'est. Quelques cupules sont reliées entre elles par une rigole. Ces rigoles suivent toujours la déclivité de la roche et n'affectent que les roches inclinées. Elles se terminent parfois en un déversoir en bordure du bloc gravé. Elles ont certainement servi à drainer un liquide.

Nous assimilons ces cupules (gravées) aux ponctuations (peintes), ces dernières pouvant également être isolées ou en groupes, disposées en alignements ou non organisées. Or, le point nous semble constituer l'aboutissement d'un processus de simplification du signe soléiforme. Il lui arrive en effet de participer à l'élaboration de figures solaires. Les cupules elles-mêmes sont parfois disposées en cercle ou bien servent de point de départ à des incisions rayonnantes : bloc G5,2 de Creysseilles, par exemple.

Les signes cruciformes sont nombreux et variés avec des branches égales ou inégales. Les extrémités des branches peuvent se terminer par une cupule, par un trait court transversal ou bien un cercle.

La disposition réfléchie des croix est plus nette que celle des cupules. Sur un même rocher, on peut constater des alignements ou des compositions circulaires. Ces croix sont indifféremment gravées sur des rochers aux surfaces supérieures horizontales ou obliques. Nous n'avons remarqué aucune orientation préférentielle, des rochers ou des croix.

Nous considérons la croix comme le signe dérivé de la figure anthropomorphe. Le rocher G2,2 nous en donne un bon exemple. La croix devient donc un signe anthropomorphe masculin. Le trait simple en serait l'extrême schématisation.

Le signe en arceau n'existe que dans la zone orientale. Il se présente partout sous la même forme sauf sur le rocher OR.17 où il n'est, par deux fois, qu'un simple accent épousant la moitié de la circonférence d'une cupule. Ce signe est issu de la figure dite de l'idole. Les étapes de sa simplification ont été mises en évidence par de nombreux auteurs (Glory 1948, Bellin 1959, Hameau, 1989, 2003) C'est la forme extérieure de cette figure qui a été privilégiée ici dans le processus de schématisation.

Nous observons à Creysseilles le doublement presque systématique du signe en arceau, comme cela existe sur de nombreux sites, gravés ou peints. Le doublement de l'idole est un fait récurrent dans l'expression schématique du Néolithique (Hameau 2002, 2003) Nous estimons que ce doublement est d'ordre sémantique et n'est pas à expliquer en termes de chronologie relative comme cela est souvent avancé (Abelanet 1986).

Les autres signes sont très peu nombreux : trois petits cercles piquetés (OR.16) et une hache supposée (G2,3). L'identification d'un oiseau sur le rocher OR.07 (Bellin 1978) ne résulte que de la forme du tracé de la rigole centrale.

Les thèmes

Les figures répertoriées à Creysseilles constituent les éléments d'un corpus homogène mais réduit à trois figures principales : le signe soléiforme dans sa version simplifiée de cupule, le signe anthropomorphe masculin à divers stades de sa schématisation (personnage masculin, signe cruciforme à branches égales ou inégales, simple trait) et l'idole réduite à la représentation d'un arceau. Cette réduction du corpus est conforme à ce que nous observons sur tous les sites ornés où l'exubérance de la décoration résulte en fait de la répétition des mêmes catégories de figures sous des versions graphiques différentes. A Creysseilles, les cupules et signes assimilés dominent très largement: 81,2%, suivies des signes anthropomorphes (13,5%) et de l'idole (4,2%). L'ensemble des autres signes représente 1%. Ces chiffres sont identiques à ceux tirés du répertoire pictural schématique du sud de la France où les ponctuations représentent près des 4/5 de l'ensemble du corpus, suivies de très loin par les représentations anthropomorphes et l'idole. Ce qui différencie essentiellement le corpus iconographiques gravé du même peint, en France méridionale, est la plus grande schématisation des signes et l'absence d'animaux dans le premier (Hameau, 2006).

Les thèmes résultent de l'association des signes selon deux principes qui sont la juxtaposition ou la contraction. A Creysseilles, les trois signes se combinent, soit par leur doublement, soit par leur association deux par deux, soit par leur rapprochement en une triade. Ainsi, la cupule ou le signe cruciforme, ou encore l'arceau peuvent être doublés. La cupule peut accompagner le signe cruciforme ou l'arceau. Les trois signes peuvent être réunis sur un même support. En cas de doublement, le doublement est souvent imparfait : un signe est plus petit que l'autre, un signe est de morphologie différente de l'autre, un seul des deux signes est accompagné d'une cupule. Enfin, les figures ont une charge sémantique différente en fonction de leur sens de lecture : droit, couché ou inversé. Toutes ces combinaisons sont présentes à Creysseilles.

Les thèmes sont également perceptibles par l'agencement des figures sur leur support. Les signes s'ordonnent en registres haut/bas ou gauche/droit. Ainsi, sur le rocher OR.01 dit des "Pieds du Diable" quatre registres se succèdent (Fig. 9.2c). De haut en bas, nous avons deux idoles, puis deux signes anthropomorphes différemment tracés dont un est accompagné de cupules, puis deux idoles dont une est ponctuée, puis une idole en position couchée. Cette combinaison de signes, doublés, ponctués et/ou inversés est présente sous des versions plus ou moins complètes sur d'autres sites gravés ou peints : le Castellet d'Arles, le plateau du Daüs à Mercuer (Ardèche), le Signal de la Lichère à Branoux (Gard), les rochers des Vaux à Saint-Aubin de Baubigné (Deux-Sèvres), la grotte Dumas à Ollioules (Var), la grotte Chuchy à Tourves (Var), etc.

Conception et utilisation du sanctuaire

Si l'on considère l'ensemble du site, seule la zone orientale du sanctuaire correspond vraiment à cette combinaison des trois catégories de figures. Creysseilles occidental ne présente en effet que des personnages masculins et des signes soléiformes et l'idole n'y est pas intégrée à la thématique. La distinction des deux zones semble donc spatiale et sémantique à la fois : une zone où le discours ne porte que sur l'homme et une autre où l'idole, souvent considérée comme un intercesseur, intervient par rapport à ce dernier.

Cependant, l'importance du nombre des figures et des supports gravés à Creysseilles nous amène à supposer une longue fréquentation du sanctuaire. Dans ce cas, plusieurs stratégies spatiales sont possibles : ajouter de nouvelles figures au côté des précédentes ou bien agrandir la surface à graver. Même dans la longue durée, la division sémantique des deux zones a été préservée. Même si l'on a rajouté des figures sur des supports déjà gravés, l'idole n'a été représentée que dans la zone orientale. Par contre, il semble qu'on ait rajouté des supports dans la zone occidentale puisque 17 rochers n'y sont pas solidaires du substrat, tous placés en arrière du rebord du plateau, et ces rochers ont été majoritairement ornés de cupules. Or, sur de nombreux sites, peints ou gravés, nous avons montré que le point ou la cupule, seuls, occupent la périphérie de l'espace investi par l'expression schématique (Hameau, à paraître). Nous proposons de considérer ces rochers déplacés comme autant de supports liés à un usage prolongé du sanctuaire. Nous pensons même que la thématique des rochers les plus à l'ouest de la zone orientale, uniquement gravés de cupules, répond de la même stratégie d'ajouts postérieurs aux autres supports rupestres (Fig. 9.1b).

LES REUTILISATIONS DU SANCTUAIRE

Les deux corniformes

Sur la face latérale nord du rocher H7.4, on observe deux figures corniformes (Fig. 9.2d). Ces signes ont été exécutés après mise en forme du rocher puisqu'ils se superposent à quelques encoches obliques. Ils sont réalisés par piquetage de la roche. Il s'agit de deux formes trapézoïdales pleines poursuivies, de chaque côté, par des appendices, longs et décrivant un angle droit. Ce sont les seules figures de ce type et réalisées selon cette technique sur le site de Creysseilles. Elles n'appartiennent pas au corpus précédemment étudié. Nous les rapprochons des bucranes gravés sur les pentes du Mont Bégo (Alpes-Maritimes), par exemple. Elles en ont en effet la forme et la technique.

On connaît des manifestations d'un "culte taurin" dès l'extrême fin du Vème millénaire av. J.C. (Le Roux, 1992). Il réapparaît en France au début des âges des Métaux. Certaines figures schématiques peintes de la Péninsule ibérique présentent des appendices cornus qui semblent indiquer qu'un fond de croyance ayant trait au bovidé subsiste dans l'art tout au long du Néolithique. Le sud du Portugal restitue, au Chalcolithique, des sanctuaires rupestres où abondent des corniformes proches des nôtres (Gomes, 1991).

Nous n'avons aucun moyen de dater les deux figures cornues de Creysseilles. Seule la marginalisation de ces figures milite en faveur de leur postériorité aux cupules du même rocher.

L'art schématique linéaire

Douze témoins d'une réutilisation plus tardive du sanctuaire ont également été trouvés sur la seule partie occidentale du site: 11 moellons gravés de fines incisions et quatre lignes brisées réalisées avec le même trait fin sur le rocher H7.2. Les figures sur moellons sont des grilles et des marelles, des figures rayonnantes, des lignes brisées et des traits fins sans organisation apparente (Fig. 9.2e). Tous ces supports sont de petite taille, prismatiques ou parallélépipédiques, et en basalte. Le choix du matériau est donc manifeste.

Neuf de ces blocs ont été trouvés en étroite relation avec les rochers cupulés, au pied de ceux-ci. Nous pensons que les blocs étaient posés sur les cupules elles-mêmes, à l'origine. Dans le cas des rochers H3.3 et I5.2, gravés d'une cupule centrale de grand diamètre, les blocs de basalte ont été retrouvés posés sur cette cupule, face gravée tournée vers le bas. Dans le cas de H3.3, la cupule était cachée par six pierres disposées en étoiles au-dessus d'un remplissage de sable (désagrégation du grès) : quatre pierres de grès et deux blocs en roche volcanique gravés. Nous constatons donc à Creysseilles, l'association délibérée des blocs finement incisés avec des rochers uniquement ornés de cupules. Les associations de signes sont donc par neuf fois celle d'une marelle avec une cupule et par quatre fois celle d'un signe rayonnant avec une cupule.

Aucun argument de terrain ne permet vraiment de dater ces fines gravures : contemporaines des cupules ou plus tardives ? Leur découverte en étroite relation avec les cupules indiquerait à première vue des expressions artistiques synchrones. Le matériau choisi pourrait être un argument pour une différence chronologique. En effet, si les incisions fines sont sur blocs de basalte, nous avons signalé la découverte de deux petits blocs de grès monocupulaires. A chaque période et à chaque corpus iconographique correspondrait sa roche.

Une étude technique et stylistique nous fait penser que ces gravures appartiennent à l'art schématique linéaire qui se caractérise par des personnages et des signes figurés selon un processus de schématisation en tous points semblable à celui qui est en usage dès le Néolithique mais réalisés par incision superficielle du support. Cet art couvre une zone étendue, de la Péninsule ibérique à tout l'arc alpin. Sa datation reste cependant délicate. Les premières manifestations linéaires ne remontent pas au-delà du II ème siècle av. J.C. Son *terminus ante quem* est plus difficile à cerner puisque des manifestations de cet art datent visiblement du Moyen-Age (Campmajo 1984, 2005) et que des survivances sont décelables jusqu'au début du XXème siècle (Hameau, 1994, 2001).

La reprise des sanctuaires préhistoriques par l'art linéaire est chose courante. Pour le sud de la France sont concernés tant des abris peints que des sanctuaires gravés. L'art linéaire se superpose aux anciens signes, est exprimé à proximité immédiate de ceux-ci, ou investit un lieu très proche. Il est discret lorsque les manifestations artistiques antérieures sont nombreuses et s'affirme avec force dans le cas contraire. Cet effet d'équilibre nous fait supposer que les lieux ornés à la fin du Néolithique n'ont jamais vraiment cessé d'être des lieux sacrés à défaut d'être des lieux utilisés en permanence pour des pratiques cultuelles. Cet ancien usage s'est poursuivi ou du moins a été connu jusqu'aux périodes historiques.

CONCLUSION

Le site de Creysseilles nous apparaît donc comme un sanctuaire important par le nombre des supports utilisés pour la gravure. Cette ampleur nous a permis de faire la part de l'organisation du site et celle de sa fréquentation. L'hypothèse d'une partition sémantique est appuyée sur la nature même du sanctuaire, divisé en deux espaces différemment agencés et ornés. Cette supposition résulte d'une analyse qui prend en compte le rapport site/support/signe en tant qu'emboîtement d'espaces iconographiques. Un regroupement de gravures rupestres n'est concevable et analysable que dans la complémentarité de ses supports et de ses figures, que dans une recherche d'une cohérence de l'ensemble des rochers investis par l'expression graphique.

Nous observons donc l'existence de deux ensembles iconographiques : à l'ouest, une zone qui n'exprime que le personnage masculin associé ou non à la cupule, cette dernière ajoutant du sens à la présence du premier, et à l'est, une zone où l'idole transforme la relation des deux autres figures. Nous pourrions supposer la distinction entre l'expression d'un monde terrestre et celle d'un monde supranaturel attesté par l'existence de l'idole. Cette dichotomie se serait perpétuée tout au long du Néolithique, la fréquentation du site se matérialisant par l'apport de nouveaux supports et le respect des thématiques mises en place et de leur répartition spatiale.

Comment et à quel titre, les corniformes du rocher H7.4 s'intègrent-ils dans cet ensemble ? Comment expliquer les réminiscences tardives que sont les témoignages d'art schématique linéaire, réminiscences réglementées si l'on en juge leur respect du corpus ancien ? Nous ne pouvons que constater leur existence et la perpétuation d'une double "nature" du sanctuaire. Cette division bipartite du site semble attestée par la microtoponymie qui place la zone occidentale du côté des forces positives, des Croix de Saint-André, et qui désigne les arceaux de l'idole par le terme de Pieds-du-Diable: résultat bien connu d'une tentative de "christianisation" des lieux.

References

ABELANET, J. (1986) - *Signes sans paroles, cent siècles d'art rupestre en Europe occidentale*. Paris: Ed. Hachette- Coll. "la Mémoire du Temps". 345 p.

ABELANET, J. (1990) - *Les roches gravées nord catalanes*. Perpignan : Centre d' Etudes Préhistoriques Catalanes. 209 p.

BELLIN, P. (1959) - Schématisme méditerranéen en Ardèche. *Bulletin de la Société Préhistorique Française*. Paris t. LVI, n°9-10, p.521-529.

BELLIN, P. et al. (1978) - Nouvelles stations d' art schématique de la Drôme, de l'Ardèche et de l'Isère, *Bulletin d'Etudes Préhistoriques Alpines*, Aoste t.X, p.113-151.

CAMPMAJO, P.; UNTERMANN, J. (1984) - Les gravures rupestres linéaires de la Cerdagne française. In *6ème Colloqqui Internacional d'Arqueologia de Puigcerdà*, p.317-336

CAMPMAJO, P. (2005) - Les gravures ibères dans l'art rupestre de l'âge du fer, le cas de la Cerdagne (Pyrénées-Orientales). In *Mon Ibèric als països catalans, volum II. XIIIe Colloqui Internacional d'Arqueologia de Puigcerdà*. Puigcerdà: Institut d'Estudis Ceretans, p.1101-1133.

GLORY, A.; SANZ-MARTINEZ, J.; GEORGEOT, P.; NEUKIRCH H. (1948) - Les peintures de l'âge du métal en France Méridionale, *Préhistoire* Toulouse, t.X, p.7-135.

GOMES, M. V. (1991) - Les corniformes de deux sanctuaires rupestres dans le sud du Portugal, Chronologie et interprétation. In *Pré-Actes du Colloque "Le Mont Bégo"*, Tende, juillet 1991, t.1, p.434-496.

HAMEAU, P. (1989) - *Les Peintures Postglaciaires en Provence (Inventaire, étude chronologique, stylistique et iconographique)*, Documents d'Archéologie Française n°22, Paris, 124p.

HAMEAU, P. (1994) - Les gravures de la bastide de Cambaret (Brignoles). *Art Rupestre*. Milly-la-Forêt n°40, p.21-28.

HAMEAU, P. (1999) - Héliotropisme et hygrophilie des abris à peintures schématiques du sud de la France. *L'Anthropologie*. Paris. 103, n°4, p.617-631.

HAMEAU, P. (2001) - L'art schématique linéaire dans le Sud-Est de la France - *Anthropologie*. Paris. 105, p.565-610.

HAMEAU, P. (2002) - *Passage, transformation et art schématique: l'exemple des Peintures néolithiques du sud de la France*. Oxford : British Archaeological Reports, vol. 1044 , 280p. 204 fig.

HAMEAU, P. (2003) - Que l'idole est antérieur à l'homme ... *Revue du Centre Archéologique du Var*. Toulon, *2003*, p.35-42.

HAMEAU, P. (2006) - Animal et expression schématique néolithique dans le sud de la France: entre réel et idéel, Anthropozoologica. Paris, 41 (2), p.513-537.

HAMEAU, P. (à paraître) - Un vaste sanctuaire de plein-air: Le Signal de la Lichère (Branoux-les-Taillades, Gard). In *Colloque Préhistoire des Causses*, Millau juin 2005, à paraître.

LE ROUX, C.T. (1992) - Cornes de Pierres ... *Revue Archéologique de l'Ouest*. Nantes, Supplément n°5, p.237-244.

SYMBOLISME DU METAL: UN PROPOSITION DE REFLEXION SUR LES DEPOTS DU B.F. IIIB DE LA REGION P.A.C.A.

Davide DELFINO

I.I.S.L. – Institute International d' Etudes Liguriennes, section Valbormida, Italy

Abstract: In the area of "metallurgical circle of the Westerns Alps", many depots are presents in the Late Brozne Age IIIb: 9 of these are interpretables as riches votives depositions with objects bindeds to horseman's panoply. In this time the region see the birth of an association of two culturals groups, natives and migrants from the Isere's and Savoyan's plateaux. This last show an strong obstentation of his metallurgical craftmanschip and traditons of late past, witch is visible in votives depositions. This archaeological clearness give an possibility to make an cognitiv study to understand the simbolism of holy, of the inteaction with the territory, but also of cultural heritage ad ethinc identification.
Keywords: metallurgy, symbolism, ethnic identity, study of depots

Résumè: Dans le contexte de la "cercle metallurguique des Alpes de l'Ouest", beaucoup de depots sont y presents au B.F. IIIb: 9 de ceux ci, sont sonsiderables offrands votifs très riches avec d'objects liès à panoplies de chevalier. En meme temp, cette region voie la naissance d' une association des deux groupes culturels, autoctones et migrantes des plateaux de l'Isère et de la Savoye. Ces dernièrs montrent une fort obstentation du leur l'artisanat du metal et des traditions du recent passè, qui sont visibles dans le depots votifs,. Ces depositions donnent la possibilitè de commencer un ètude cognitive pour comprendre la symbologie de sacralitè, d' interaction avec le territoir, mais aussi de conservation culturelle et d'identification etnique.
Mots clés: metallurgie, symbolisme, identitè ethnique, etude des depots.

LA CERCLE METALLURGIQUE DES ALPES OCCIDENTALS AU B.F. IIIB: ENCARREMENT ET PERSPECTIVS D' INTERPRETATION DES METAUX

Durant l' age du Bronze Final dans les Alpes françaises se developpe la cercle metallurgique des Alpes de l' ouest, caracterisèe par une elevè dynamicitè d'assimilation des models d'objects metalliques par des areennes ètrangeres et pour originalitè dans leur re-elaboration. Cette manifestation, commence durant le Bronze Finale I[1] quand la region alpine et les plateaux pre-alpins connaisent une bonne production d'objets metalliques, avec caracteres typiquement local[2], subdivisèes en macroregions de production. Au Bronze Final III il y a maintenant soit dans les regions alpins que dans les plateaux un vif artisanat du bronze avec caracteres typiques des respectives communautèes des metallurgues: dans les plateaux on y peut voir les production du type lacustres[3], et dans les alpes des productions qui sont influencèes par des models importès de l' Italie.

La production metallurgique voit ici son *maximum*, avec des importations des models etrangers et leur nouvelle elaboration dans les Alpesarrive aussi à un considerable accroissement de la production d'objects metalliques[4].

En ce cadre dans la macroregion des Alpes de l'ouest on y peut voir l'arrive au Bronze Final IIIb des peuples habitants les plateaux pre alpines de la Savoye et de l'Isère que se poussent vers l'interieur des vallèes alpins,

phenomene peut etre aussi liè au changement climatique du debut du sub-atlantique[5], que portait un abbaissement de temperature et une augmentation d' umiditè: ce nouveau climat rendrait possible l'installation d' un economie rurale dans les region à l'interieur des Alpes avec la naissance des communautèes rurals que developpent la tradition artiginal du metal. Liè à cette activitè, un autre motif de ces mouvements c'est l'exploitation des ressources metalliphères alpines[6]. Dans ce periode les vallèes alpines sont tres peuplèes et y se developpent des nouvelles communautèes qui portrent leur respectives traditions, visible dans l'artisanat du bronze, qui rest le temoignage plus evident d' eux: en particulier, on y peut voir des symbolismes liè aux traditions des nouveaux arrivèes. Les metals pour la plus part furent trouvès dans des depots, qui sont des bonnes contexts pour étudier le symbolisme du metal par l'analys des types presents (combien par type? Quels types? Pourquoi des types et non des autres?)

LES DEPOTS DES REGIONS ALPINS INTERIEURES DE PROVENCE-ALPES-COTE D'AZUR

Etude des depots

Les depots qui ont enteret pour notre recherche, sont lequels de la region P.A.C.A.[7], et entre eux lequels qui sont bien connues, ceux-qui continennent d'objects de typologie bien definie. Pour une bonne analyse, on a utilisè une metode de fichement des depots, qui prévoit des voix à compiler lesquelles donnent les informations

---

[1] En cronologie de Hatt.
[2] Bocquet, Lebascle 1983.
[3] Kerouanton I. 1998.
[4] Bocquet, Lebascle 1983.
[5] Bocquet A. 1991 et Morin 1999.
[6] Bocquet A. 1991.
[7] Provence-Alpes-Cote d' Azur.

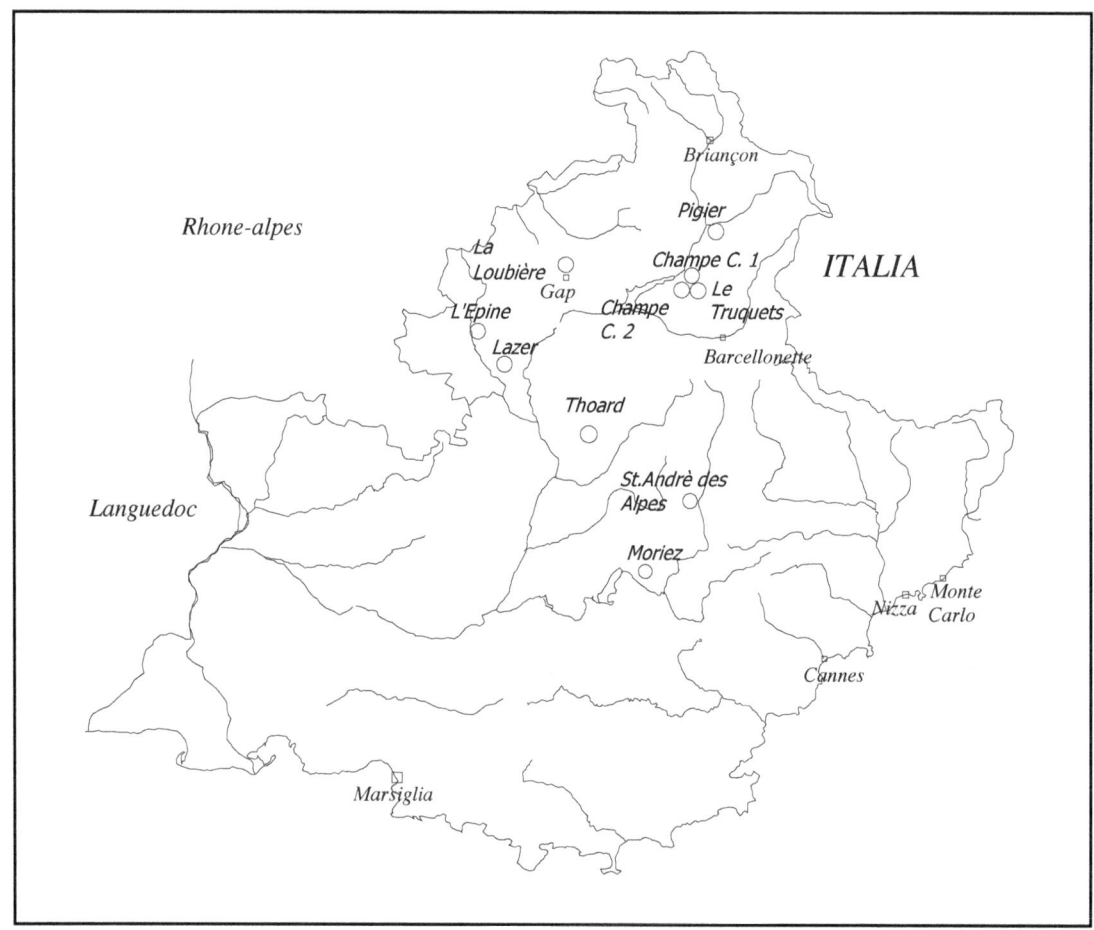

Fig. 10.1. Distribution des depots etudiès en la region P.A.C.A.

necessaires puor elaborer une interpretation du depot (finalisès au stokage de produits finies, stokage d'objects à refondre, ou offrands votifs), qui est l'objectif du fichement. Les voix sont:

1) Modalitè de decouvert 2) Objects et leur etat de conservation 3) Confrontation typologique des objects 4) Cronologie du depot 5) Collocation dans la region du depot 6) Bibliographie

Malheuresement il n'y a pas d'espace ici pour montrer toutes les fiches elaborès pour tous les 10 depots etudiès, qui sont: (Fig. 10.1)

1. Moriez, S. Andrè des Alpes, Thoard pour les ALPES-DE-HAUTE-PROVENCE

2. La Loubière, Champe Colombe 1, Champe Colombe 2, Le Truquets, L' Epine, Pigier et Lazer pour les HAUTES ALPES

Interpretation des depots

La majoritè des ces depots peuvent etre enterpretès comme depositions votifs: à l' enterieur d'eux il y a d'objects selectionnès par type et presque toujours intacts, à l'exception des quelques-uns qui sont damnagè par les travailles de recouvrement des depots (un exemple peut etre Moriez[8]); ils sont en lieux presque en zones isolès et qui ne permittent pas d' eux recouvrer. Peux d'autres depots ne sont pas definible surement comme votifs et un seul et caracterisable comme depots de stokage:

– Offrandes votifs

En ce goupe il y a les depots de Champe Colombe 1[9] et 2[10], St. Andrè des Alpes[11], Moriez[12] et Guillestre[13]: Champe Colombe 2 e Guillestre sont chez le gre d'un torrent , Champe Colombe 1 sur la rive d' un torrent[14] et St. Andrè des Alpes dans une probable tombe à tumul[15]; pour Moriez les objects presents et les modalitès de decouvrement, font enteprenter ce depots comme offrand votiv[16]. En tous il y a d'objects presque intacts, et si nous

---

[8] Barge H. 2004.
[9] Chantre 1875-76; Muller 1991; Barruol, Bertucchi 1995; Haussmann 1996; Garcia 2003; Barge 2004.
[10] Muller 1991; Barruol, Bertucchi 1995; Garcia 2003; Barge 2004.
[11] Olivier 1884-1886; Eluere 1982; Barge 2004; Garcia 2003.
[12] Barge H., Haussmann L. 1997; Garcia 1995, 2001; Martin 2001; H. Barge 2004, I Liguri 2004.
[13] Courtois 1960; Muller 1991; Barruol, Bertucchi 1995; Garcia 2003; Barge 2004.
[14] Qui peut etre ètè le grè du cours d'eau en temps anciennes.
[15] Garcia D. 2003.
[16] Barge H. 2004.

Tab. 10.1. Les objects communes aux depots.

Depot	FAL.	CINT.	APPL.	ARM.	PEND.	BOT.	TORQ.	GR. PEND.	P. RUOTE.
Guillestre	1	1	–	1	–	–	–	–	–
Le Truquets	–	1	–	–	15	4	21	2	–
Champe C. 1	1	–	32	20	9	55	–	–	4
Champe C. 2	–	–	–	–	–	–	–	–	–
La Loubière	1	1	–	2	–	2	5	–	3
Thoard	18	–	–	–	–	18	1	–	–
St. A.des Alpes	4	–	–	18	–	20	2	–	–
Moriez	12	–	–	2	49	–	5	3	3
L' Epine	2	–	–	12	9	–	–	–	2
Lazer	2	–	18	–	–	15	–	–	–

Abreviations: FAL.= Falères; CINT. = Ceintures; APPL. = Appliques; ARM. = Armilles; PEND. = Pendeloques; BOT. = Boutons; TORQ. = Torques; GR. PEND. = Grands Pendentifs; P. RUOTE = Pendentifs à rouelles.

voyons les depositions votifs comme les *gewasserfunde* qui ont des objects fragmentès on y peut voir une contraddition: mais c'est toutefois vrai que on peut deposer une offrande aussi en la confiand à des lieux inaccessibles à la place de la rompre.

– *Offrands votifs probables*

Trois depots ne sont pas identifiables surement comme offrands votifs: bien que à La Loubière[17] on y a des objects caracterisables comme offrand, pour ce depot n' avons suffisants information sur son lieux et condition de gisement; pour Thoard[18] et Les Trouchets[19] aussi nous avons les memes problemes d' interpretation et c'est toujours dangereux la faire avec trop d' hate. Esuite pour le depot de Lazer[20] aussi nous ne savons pas non plus le lieux où il etait decouvrè, peut etre le grè d'un torrent[21].

– *Depositions non votifs*

En ce group il y a seulement le depot de L' Epine[22], qui il s'agit d'une deposition recouvrable, en etant dans un lieu faisablement accessible et avec les objects conservès dans un pot.

Analys et interpretation degs objects communes aux depots de P.A.C.A. (Tab. 10.1)

Dans les depots etudiès, on y a des objects de parure qui sont communes à la region de P.A.C.A., qui peutent etre considerès ensuite comme une production typique local:

entre eux il y a des types qui ont des caracteristiques utiles pour observer un symbolisme des depositions.

– *Les faleres* (Fig. 10.2)

Sont en 8 depots sur 10; peutent etre ensuite un classe d'objetcs très diffusè sur le territoire et sont particulières des depots alpins de cette region au B.F. IIIb: Moriez et Champtercier en ont en nombre considerable. Les motifs decoratifs sont très communes à tous les exemplaires: cerlces concentriques, souvent avec motifs à etoile ou à points. Comme a dejà observè H. Barge[23] sont des produits des ateliers locaux. Mais quel signifiè ont, en depositions pour la majoritè votifs?: Kossak en les annès' 50 du siecle passè adfirmait que les exemplaires des faleres du Premièr Age du Fer du Sud-Est de l'Allemand peutent etre eteès une heritage des civilisations des *plateaux* suisses de l'Age du Bronze Final[24]. En etant des dynamiques similes en P.A.C.A., avec peuples des *plateaux* migrants vers les Alpes au B.F. IIIb, pourrait etre valide la meme intepretation pour les faleres des Hautes Alpes et Alpes de Haute Provence.

– *Les armilles*

Sont le second group d' objects communes dans les depots examinèes; appartiennent à plusieurs typologies, toutes typiques de la production des Alpes Françaises du B.F: IIIb, mais sont diffusès en toute la France du Sud Est, pas seulement en la region P.A.C.A.[25]

– *Les boutons*

Ces objects n'ont pas en eux memes un signifiè symbolique, mais en etants associès à des panoplies de chevalier, dans les depositions peutent etre considerès

---
[17] Cotte 1924; Courtois 1960; Muller 1991; Garcia 2003; Barge 2004.
[18] Olivier 1888-86; Barge 2004.
[19] Courtois 1960; Muller 1991; Haussmann 1996; Garcia 2003; Barge 2004.
[20] Muller 1991; Barruol, Bertucchi 1995; Haussmann 1997; Garcia 2003; Barge 2004.
[21] Garcia D. 2003.
[22] Courtois 1960; Cardenoux-Courtois 1979; Muller 1991; Garcia 2003; Barge 2004.

[23] Barge H. 2003.
[24] Cit. par Barge H., Kossac G. 1953.
[25] Bocquet, Lebascle 1983.

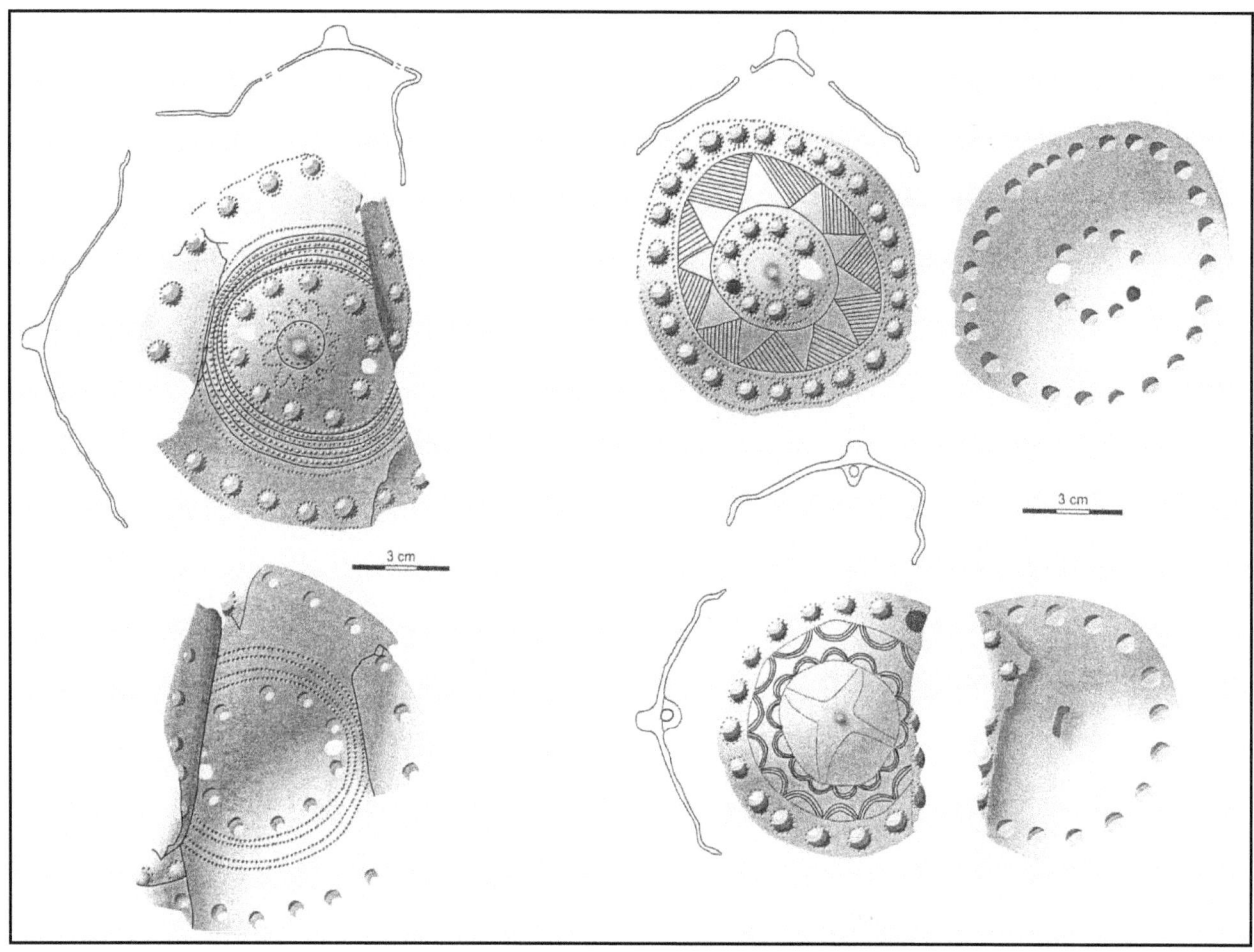

Fig. 10.2. Les phalères de Moriez (par Barge H. 2004).

comme part d'un group d'objects d'apparat avec un potentielle symbolisme liè au cheval.

– *Les torques*

Pour la majorité du type tortillè, sont dans 5 depots sur 10, et sont diffusès pas seulement en la region alpine, mais aussi dans l' Italie, l'Allemand et la Suisse. Mais les torques des Alpes de Haute Provence ont une particularitè: les anneuax enfilès dans eux, qui peuvent avoir une fonction sonore, comme la quelle hypothesè pour les grands pendentifs complex[26], ou aussi de support pour des petits pendentifs, souvent retrouveès dans les depots mais separèes des torques. Cette fonction sonore peut etre associè à des motivations rituels, et peut mettre en relation les torques avec les ceintures et les grands pendentifs complexes, ayant aussi eux des elements fonctionnels pour produire un cliquetis avec les mouvements de la personne qui les revetait.

– *Les pendentifs*

Entre les types de pendentifs, sont très diffusès lesquels triangulaires: à Moriez, St. Andrè des Alpes, Champ Colombe 1 et Le Truquets. Interpretables comme elèments de ceinture, peutent etre part d'un apparat liè aux chevaux, comme des harnais. Aussi, la forme triangulaire avec un anneau, comme observait J.C. Courtois[27], peut reconduire à des protòmes de cygne schèmatisès: leur prèsence, en depositions probablement lièes au culte des eaux souligne un caractèr sacré des panoplies de chevalier, en fayant les assurer un symbolisme particulier.

– *Les rouelles*

Assez diffusèes dans les depots examinès, ont une tradition qui remonte au Bronze Antique et continue jusq' à l'Age de La Tène en toute Europe: ensuite ne sont pas particulières des Alpes Françaises, mais sont surement des objects qui rappelent le disque solaire[28] et donc qui donnent du sacré à les depots avec parures de chevalier.

– *Les ceintures* (Fig. 10.3)

Ces riches objects de parure sont seulement en trois depots, mais semblent particuliers de cette regione alpine.

---

[26] Barge H. cit, Courtois J.C. 1960.

[27] Courtois J.C. 1960.
[28] Kerouanton 1998.

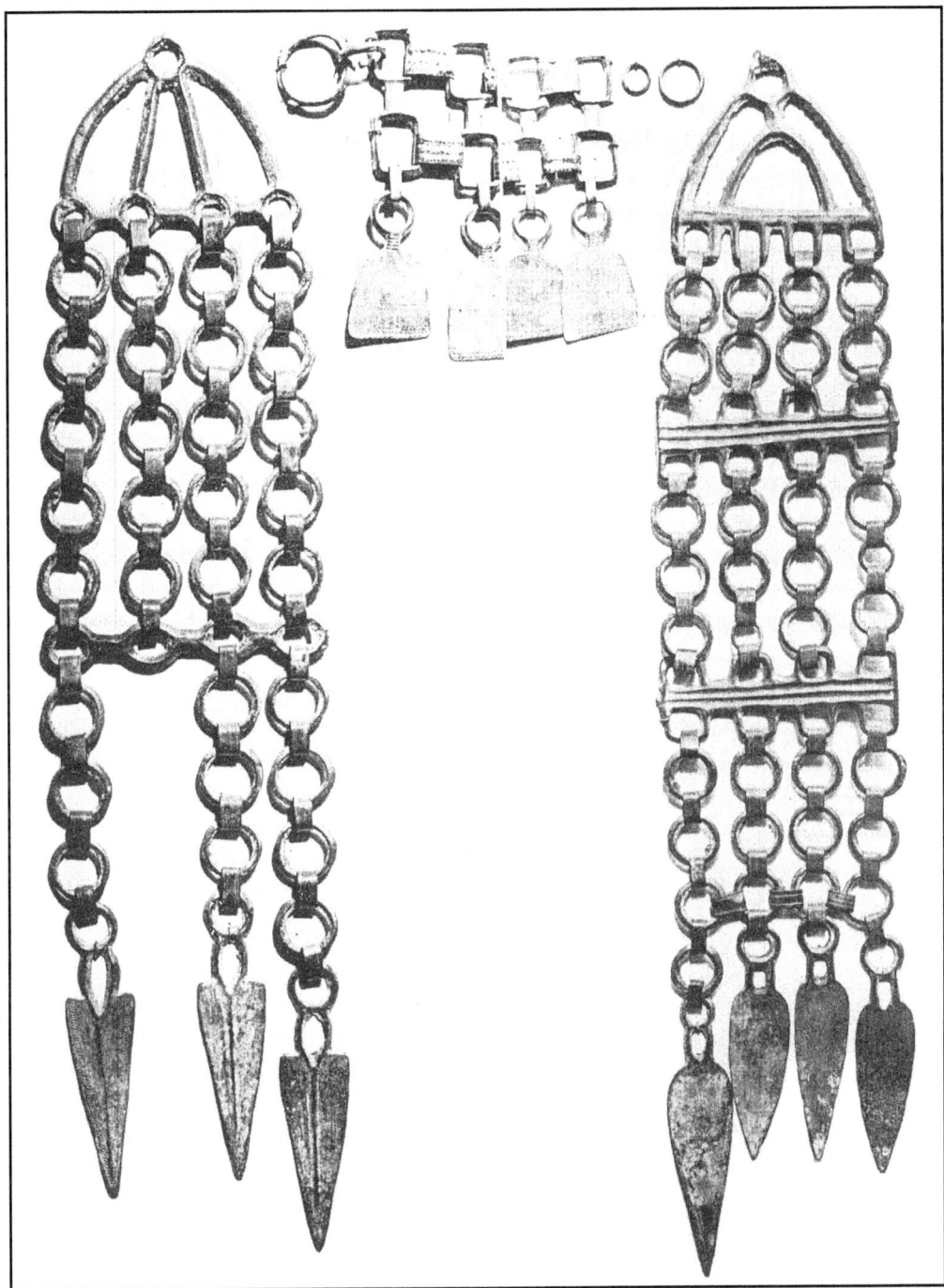

Fig. 10.3. La parure avec ceinture de La Loubière (par Courtois J.C. 1960).

Avec ses pendeloques, produisaient un cliquetis avec le mouvement de qui les revetait[29]. Il s'agit donc d' ornements cerimonials, mais aussi pour des parades et, vue les lieux de deposition, le cliquetis peut etre liè à des processions à cheval pendant le cultes des eaux.

– *Les grands pendentivs* (Fig. 10.4)

Les quels des depositions à Le Truquets et Moriez sont interpretès comme part des harnais de cheval, positionnès au collet du cheval et fayants part d' un apparat cerimonial apparu vers le X- IX siecle a.C.[30]. Ils aussi produisaient un cliquetis avec le mouvement. Ensuite ensemble à les ceintures et les falères, sont parts d'un apparat chevalin cerimonial, comme déjà plusieurs ont mis en evidence[31], mais sourtout sont des objects très riches qui bien se convient à porter un symbolisme d'obstentation des traditions ethiniques passè lieès au cheval.

---

[29] Courtois J.C. 1960.

[30] Barge H. 2004.

[31] Entre tous les auteurs: H. Barge e D. Garcia.

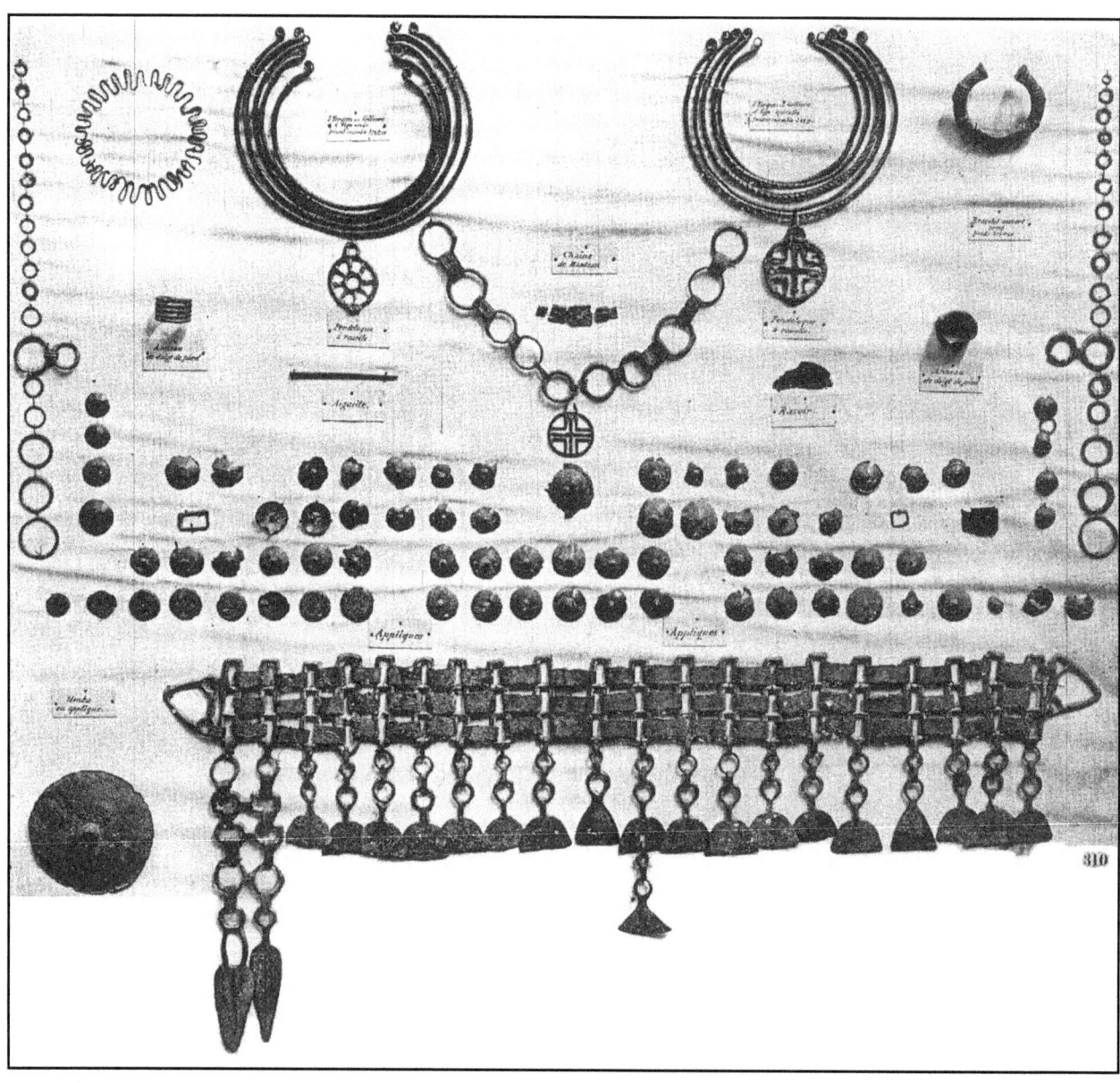

Fig. 10.4. Les grandspenentifs de Les Trouquets (par Courtois J.C. 1960).

SYMBOLISME' DES DEPOSITIONS AVEC PANOPLIE DE CHEVALIER

Cinq types d'objects peuvent etre considereès comme porteurs d'un symbolisme ethnique et culturel: le falere, le cinture articuliès, les grands pendentifs, les pendentifs et les rouelles solaires.

Tous, sauf ces dernières, sont reconduisables à riches panoplies de chevalier, objects d'excepcionel valeur, à jujer de leur lavoration[32] et de leur presence en depots votifs, chargès d' un particulier message: doner visibilitè à deux caracteristiques cultuelles et de tradition des communautès des metalurgues parvenues dans les Alpes au B.F. IIIb, liès aux activitè economiques du present et du passè. La premièr c'est le parfait artisanat des metaux,

du B.F.IIIb, visible dans le material qui fait par support au symbolisme liè aux activitès du passè: l'èlevage et l'usage des chevaux dans les plateaux de l'Isère et de la Savoye. Son symbol, liè aux parures de chevalier, serait un souvenir des temps recents, portè dans les nouveaux territoires. Et les elements pas de parure de chevalier comme les rouelles, sont liées maintenant à ces ci pour souligner la sacralité du cheval, du moment qu' ils 'agit d' un simbol, la rouelle, rappellant le disque sacré du soleil. En ce cas, le rappeler une activité economique qu'ennoble un groupe ethnique en employant les riches parures rituelles, peut se relier à celles manifestations d' obstentation ethniques déjà analysès pendant les etudies sur le symbolisme culturel des sèpoltures en Campania entre le Premier Age du Fer et l' Orientalisant[33]: mais pour les Alpes Françaises il s'agit d'un symblisme

---
[32] Barge H. 2004.

[33] Cuozzo M. 2000.

ethnique avec autres finalitès: montrer une prestigeuse ethnicitè pour signer sa dominance sur la nouvelle region peuplè, riche des matiers premiers et pour ceci absolument à revendiquer; et puis montrer une extraordinaire habilitè dans la lavoration du metaux comme puissance economique. Une double message avec une seule finalité, confiès à des produits metallurgiques usès pas comme objects commercials, mais comme offrands votifs riches de symbolisme: le support materiel en ce cas fonctionne comme un noble moyen de transport, pour la finesse de sa façon, pour un message de conservation et presentation des anciennes tradicitons qui, puisque liès à activitès nobles, justiquent la presence des ces groupes humaines sur le nouveaux territoir et sur ses ressources metalliphères qui servent à la continuation de leur artisanat des metaux.

References

BARGE, H. (2004) - Le depot de bronzes de Moriez. *Documents d'Archeologie Meridionale* N.°27, Marseille, p.141-170.

BARGE, H.; HAUSSMANN, L. (1997) - Moriez, Jas de Bernard. Bilan scientifique PACA 1996, AIX 1997, p. 24.

(dir.) BARRUOL, G.; BERTUCCHI, G. (1995) - *Carte archeologique de la Gaule. Les Hautes Alpes*. Paris, p.24.

BOCQUET, A. (1991) - L' archeologie de l'Age du Fer dans les Alpes Occidentales Françaises. In *Les Alpes à l'Age du Fer*. Actes du X Colloque sur l' Age du Fer, Yenne-Chambery. Paris, p.91-155.

BOCQUET, A.; LEBASCLE, M.C. (1983) - Metallurgia e relazioni culturali nell' età del bronzo finale delle Alpi del Nord francesi. Antropologia Alpina, Torino p.69.

CHANTRE, E. (1875-76) - Etudes palethonologiques dans le bassin du Rhone. Age du bronze; recherches sur l'origine de la métallurgie en France. Paris.

CHARDENOUX, M.B.; COURTOIS J.C. (1979) - Les haches dans la France Meridionale. *Prahistoriche bronzefunde*. Munchen. abt. IX, b.11.

COTTE, V. (1924) - *Documents sur la prehistoire de Provence. III- Stations neolithiques et protohistoriques*. Aix en Provence: ed. libraire A. Dragon, p. 162.

COURTOIS, J.C. (1960) - L'age du bronze dans les Hautes Alpes. Gallia prehistoire, fouilles et monuments archeoligiques en France metropolitaine, III. Paris, p. 101, fig.45.

CUOZZO, M. (2000) - Orizzonti teorici e interpretativi, tra percorsi di matrice francese, archeologia post-processuale e tendenze italiane: considerazioni e indirizzi di ricerca per lo studio delle necropoli. N. Terrenato (a cura di). Archeologia teorica, X ciclo di lezioni sulla ricerca applicata in Archeologia. Certosa di Pontignano (Siena), 9-14 Agosto 1999. Consiglio Nazionale delle Ricerche-Università di Siena, pp.323-360.

ELOUERE, C. (1992) - Deux importatnts decouverts du XIX siecle acquises par la Societè des Amis du MAN: le depot de St. Andrè de Meouilles. *Antiquitès Nationales*. Paris. 24. p. 50-58.

GARCIA, D. (1995) - Basses Gorges du Verdon. D.R.A.C.-S.R.A. Bilan scientifique, p. 45-46.

GARCIA, D. (2001) - Vallèe de l' Ubaye. D.R.A.C.-S.R.A. Bilan scientifique, p. 36-37.

GARCIA, D. (2003) - Les depots d'objets en bronze protohistoriques en Provence-Alpes-Cote d'Azur: un etat de la question. *Documents d'Archeologie Meridionale*, N.°26, Marseille, p. 377-384.

I Liguri 2004= (a cura di) SPADEA G., DE MARINIS R.C., 2004, *I Liguri; un antico popolo europeo tra il Mediterraneo e le Alpi*, parte III, schede ; catalogo della mostra, Genova 23 ottobre-23 gennaio 2004, Ed. Skyrà, p.185.

KEROUANTON, I. (1998) - La prodution metallique des stations litorales immergèes du lac du Bourget (Savoie) à l' Age du bronze Final. L'atelier du bronzier en Europe du XX siecle au VIII siecle avant notre ère. Actes du colloque international Bronze 96, Neuchatel et Dijon: production, circulation et consommation du bronze Paris, p. 87-101.

MARTIN, L. (2001) - Quinson, route departementale 11. D.R.A.C.-S.R.A. Bilan scientifique 2001, pp. 26-27.

MORIN, M. (1999) - Recherches recentes sur l'extraction du sel dans les Alpes. Les sources saleès de la Vallèe de l'Asse (Alpes de Hautes Provence). Le puits salè de Moriez. *Minaria Helvetica*. 19a, p.3-22.

MULLER, A. (1991) - L'Age du Bronze dans les Hautes Alpes. Archeologie dans les Hautes Alpes: le Musèe departemental de Gap. Gap, p. 103-129.

OLLIVIER, D. (1878) - Bronzes et parures d' argent, Saint-Vallier (Alpes Maritimes). Materiaux, IX, p.291-292.

www.ingramcontent.com/pod-product-compliance
Ingram Content Group UK Ltd.
Pitfield, Milton Keynes, MK11 3LW, UK
UKHW061213180426
11947UKWH00029B/2026